MURDER *in* HAMTRAMCK

HISTORIC CRIMES OF PASSION & COLDBLOODED KILLINGS

GREG KOWALSKI

THE
History
PRESS

Published by The History Press
Charleston, SC
www.historypress.com

Copyright © 2021 by Greg Kowalski
All rights reserved

All photos are courtesy of the Hamtramck Historical Museum.

First published 2021

Manufactured in the United States

ISBN 9781467147101

Library of Congress Control Number: 2020945808

This book is dedicated to my brother Joe; sister, Kathy; and Joanne Sobczak; and in memory of brother Jim and Mom and Dad.

We got enough shooting going around town now.

—*city councilman Joseph Kuberacki opposing a request to allow a shooting range to open in Hamtramck, October 1936*

CONTENTS

ACKNOWLEDGEMENTS

Most of the information on the cases recounted here was derived from old newspapers in the collection of the Hamtramck Historical Museum. In a number of cases, the author quotes himself, as he wrote the original news stories from the 1970s, when he covered them as a reporter and editor of the *Hamtramck Citizen* newspaper. The *New Deal* newspaper also served as a source of information, as did the *Hamtramck Times* newspaper dating to late nineteenth and early twentieth centuries. These can be found in the Library of Congress. Information about specific events, persons and the general history of Hamtramck were drawn from the extensive archives of the Hamtramck Historical Museum.

INTRODUCTION

It's all here: greed, sex, revenge, ambition, blinding anger, coldly calculated schemes and bumbling buffoons with guns, knives and bludgeons. One thing ties them together: murder—the deliberate act of taking the life of another person without proper authority. It sounds so simple, and sometimes it is. It can be as easy as the twitch of a trigger. But the effects are staggering. Futures are abruptly ended, husbands and wives become widowers and widows, children are transformed into orphans and, of course, lives are lost. Perpetrators suffer as well. Some lose their lives in committing the crime. Others are caught and spend years, as much as the remainder of their lives, in jail. A few, where the particular state itself engages in homicide, are executed.

No town is immune to murder. Crime happens everywhere, it's said. But for most of us, it's no more than a headline in a newspaper or a story on the nightly news. If it bleeds, it leads, the old news axiom goes. And we read and watch with irresistible morbid curiosity. Then we turn the page or switch the channel and the moment's thrill is gone. It's only when violence strikes you or someone you know that it becomes real.

Ever seen an actual murder victim? The experience is nothing like what you see on TV or in the movies. There's an eerie sense of stillness, of finality, in a dead body whose existence has ended by violence. It's a life interrupted permanently.

And why? That's where the story is. What were the circumstances that led to this extreme conclusion? And, of course, who did it? Often there's no mystery to the story at all. The killer is as obvious as the act. Other cases are cracked only after meticulous investigation or with the help of a lucky break. And sometimes the crime isn't solved at all. The murder of Hamtramck teen Bernice Onisko officially remains an open case today, more than eighty years after it occurred. But no matter what, it's a fascinating story, which is why we are here.

On the pages ahead, you are going to encounter a conglomerate of mayhem dating back centuries. The city of Hamtramck is not unique in that murders have taken place there from time to time, but the stories behind them are unusually fascinating. Perhaps it is the dynamics of the city with its modern roots in a massive immigrant influx and the way its character was formed by heavy industry and the peculiar culture it fostered. Maybe the intensity of living in Hamtramck was a factor, with its extreme housing density that pushed neighbor on top of neighbor, often literally. Alcohol, unemployment and poverty were also frequent factors in crime. That might seem obvious for any town, but these factors had a special impact in Hamtramck, where they were magnified beyond normal conventions. Consider that during the Great Depression the national unemployment rate was about 25 percent. In Hamtramck, because of the city's heavy reliance on the auto industry, the unemployment rate was near 60 percent. That's beyond awful. It was cataclysmic and put intense pressure on families seeking ways to just survive. Combine that with an overindulgence in alcohol, partly due to cultural heritage and partly to desperation and tragedy, which was lurking everywhere.

But while there are common threads coursing through these tales, every case is unique.

This is not a comprehensive account of every murder that has ever occurred in Hamtramck, although there has not been so many that such a compilation could not be done. Rather, this is a selective retelling of the most interesting cases. Their complexities, the impact they had other individuals and even the whole community and whatever other unusual elements that have made their details ripe for retelling are what count here. You might glean something about inhuman nature from these stories, although you'll likely be left asking "Why?" even when the killer is identified, caught and convicted.

But that's the nature of murder.

1

THE SCENE OF THE CRIME

As with any proper police investigation, we must begin by looking at where crime occurred.

In our cases, we are confined to one area, the city of Hamtramck. It's a town that sports a checkered past that it long tried to ignore, like the uncle in prison that the family pretends doesn't exist. But the past can't be changed even if dressed by a veneer of respectability. It wasn't always that way, of course. Hamtramck was born of virgin woods, nestled among the greatest collection of freshwater lakes in the world and along the banks of what would become known as *Detroit*—French for "the Straits," or Detroit River.

The Native Americans were here first and were followed by the French. In fact, Hamtramck is named after a French Canadian man, Jean Francois Hamtramck, who came to the Unites States to fight with the new American army against the British. He despised the British for their actions in the French and Indian War.

Hamtramck legally Americanized his name to John Francis Hamtramck and distinguished himself in the army. After the Revolutionary War, Hamtramck returned to the army, and in 1796, President George Washington sent him and General "Mad" Anthony Wayne to remove the British from Detroit. They stayed on American soil after the Revolution, often harassing the locals. Washington feared they might try to foment another Revolution, so the president wanted them moved out. Colonel Hamtramck's troops did that in 1796, and in 1798, when the Detroit area was first subdivided into four townships, one of them was named in his honor.

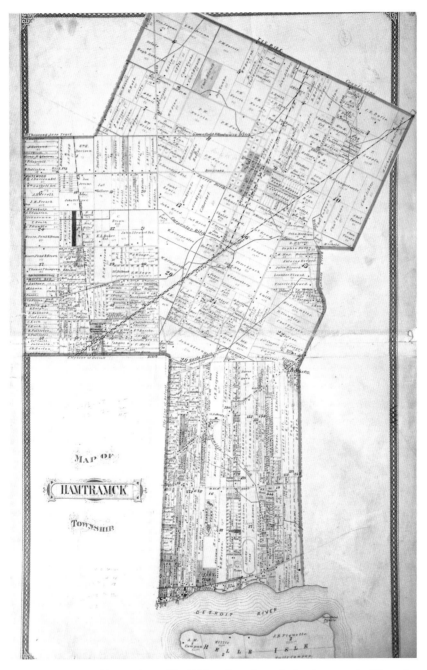

Hamtramck Township was formed in 1798 and was huge. Its borders stretched from the Detroit River on the south to about Woodward Avenue on the west to Base Line (Eight Mile Road) on the north to Lake St. Clair on the east.

Hamtramck Township was a sprawling affair. It stretched from the Detroit River to Base Line (now Eight Mile Road) and from Woodward Avenue through what would become the Grosse Pointe communities along Lake St. Clair. It was a huge area filled mainly with swamps and forests of questionable value.

Colonel Hamtramck died in 1803 at age of forty-five and was laid to rest at the graveyard of the original Sainte Anne de Detroit Church in Detroit. Later, when Sainte Anne's moved, so did the colonel, and, in fact, he was moved again later to Mount Elliott Cemetery elsewhere in Detroit. And in 1962, his weary body was uplifted once again and reinterred at Veterans Memorial Park in Hamtramck. He's still there. Stop by and say bonjour.

Through the nineteenth century, the city of Detroit grew at the expense of Hamtramck. Pieces of Hamtramck Township were carved off and added to Detroit every so often. Hamtramck Township was reformed in 1818 and 1827, but that did nothing to stop the continuing loss. Early on, the French withdrew and were replaced by German immigrant farmers, a number of whom settled in an area of the township about five miles north of the Detroit River, where a pair of railroad tracks crossed. By 1900, this had evolved into a community that adopted its own Hamtramck identity. Fearful of being completely swallowed by Detroit, representatives of the five hundred or so area residents met in 1900 in the new Holbrook School to consider officially forming the village of Hamtramck. A vote was taken, the measure was passed and the residents filed the appropriate paperwork with the State of Michigan to incorporate as a village. That was approved by the state in 1901, and chains were laid out defining an area of about 2.1 square miles. After all of that excitement, a dusty haze of tranquility settled on the sleepy little village of Hamtramck. Of course, there wasn't much for the dust to settle on—a few stores, some simple wooden houses, a few impressive wooden houses, one paint factory and an assortment of saloons. We will be discussing much more about them later.

For the next nine years, nothing of consequence happened, except the establishment of St. Florian Catholic parish in 1907. We'll hear more about that too. Detroit continued its inevitable growth, and what remained of Hamtramck Township shrank even more. Then in June 1910, two guys came into town who changed everything. Indeed, it's likely that if they hadn't come to Hamtramck, there would be no Hamtramck today. It would have been swallowed up with the rest of the area by Detroit. But John and Horace Dodge would not want that to happen, although they had no particular loyalty to Hamtramck. It was a matter of business. They were engineers,

Early Hamtramckans met in Holbrook School in 1900 to consider forming the village of Hamtramck. The school is still in use today.

The Breitmeyer farm exemplified how rural early Hamtramck was before the Dodge brothers came to town and opened their factory.

auto engineers, who were very good at what they did. After graduating from making bicycles to auto parts, they opened a factory in downtown Detroit. They built and sold auto parts to Henry Ford, who appreciated the quality of their work. So, as Ford's business grew, theirs did too. But they had bigger ideas. They didn't want to just manufacture parts. They wanted to build their own cars—something that would compete with Ford. To do that, they needed a proper factory, not a brick box crammed among the buildings in downtown Detroit, which is what they originally had. Hamtramck offered an attractive alternative. It was an independent village, meaning it had its own tax structure, which was less than Detroit's. Also, it was mainly farmland, so there was room to grow. And it was crossed by those railroad tracks, one set of which crawled up the west side of Hamtramck directly to the huge new factory that Ford had just opened in Highland Park, about a mile northwest of Hamtramck. In the short term, at least, that would be an asset. So, John and Horace bought a piece of land on Hamtramck's south end and, within four months, had some initial buildings up and were making parts for Fords.

That was just the beginning. As soon as they were able, they put out a call for new workers. That was answered in an incredible manner. Suddenly, Hamtramck was flooded with thousands of immigrants who poured into the town. Within a few years, the Dodge Brothers factory, which later became known as Dodge Main, had grown to gigantic proportions and was joined by twenty-two other factories that opened in Hamtramck. And to repeat, this was an area of just 2.1 square miles. Even more staggering was the population growth. In 1910, there were about 3,500 people living in Hamtramck. In 1920, Hamtramck's population topped 48,000, and that would reach 56,000 in 1930. Hamtramck's population growth was so steep that in 1915 the town requested that the U.S. Bureau of the Census do a special count of Hamtramck (and the neighboring city of Highland Park, which was undergoing similar, although not as radical, growth). The census found that Hamtramck was growing at a rate fifty times greater than the rest of the country.

"This remarkable growth is accounted for very largely by the greatly increased activity of the manufacturing industries within and near its borders....The manufacture of automobiles and parts constitutes by far the most important of these industries in respect to the number of persons employed," the census determined.

This phenomenal growth attracted national attention. On July 15, 1915, even the faraway *Arizona Sentinel* newspaper of Yuma, Arizona, noted:

Special Census of
Hamtramck, Michigan

A special census of the village of Hamtramck, Michigan, made at local request and expense, shows the population of that village on June 25, 1915, to have been 21,520. The increase since 1910, when the population was 3,559, has been 504 per cent. The present population comprises 21,242 whites and 278 negroes. The census was taken by local enumerators under the supervision of an official of the bureau of the Census, Eugene F. Hartley.

Hamtramck is a suburb of Detroit, lying just to the northwest of the city. Its remarkable growth is due in great measure to the presence of large automotive factories within and near its border.

Almost all of these new residents were Polish immigrants who either came straight from Poland or first settled in an eastern state, like New York or Pennsylvania, before being drawn to Hamtramck to find a job. As for the Germans who preceded the Poles and governed the town, they watched in horror as their traditional enemies from the Old Country became the dominant force in the village. Even as they contemplated this, they were faced with perhaps an even bigger problem. In 1910, when the Dodge brothers arrived, Hamtramck was still a sleepy farming town, barely developed and with lots of open space. With the creation of manufacturing jobs, the thousands of new workers drawn there needed places to live. Builders were quick to see that there was a vast market they could take advantage of. Houses, often designed for multiple families, were built on lots thirty feet wide by one hundred feet deep, leaving barely five feet of space between units. Whole blocks of houses were being built with seemingly no forethought. Wyandotte Street, two blocks south of Holbrook Avenue, was a good example of the chaos. On one unbroken street was a factory, houses, a huge high school and shops. As for the concept of zoning, forget it. The town officials certainly did. The town was a mess. Most streets were unpaved and turned into mud baths when it rained. There were no playgrounds, so the kids played in the muddy streets or the fast-disappearing empty lots. In the mid-1910s, the Hamtramck Police Department consisted of a handful of men. It was better than it had been in 1901, when two men made up the entire department. But the growth of the town made the concept of police protection questionable at best. Unsurprisingly, the village trustees were at a loss about what to do. They had founded a quiet farming town and could

The Dickinson farm was a remnant of Hamtramck's rural days, but as the town developed, farms disappeared. The Dickinson farm became the site of Dickinson School.

not have imagined that it would turn into an industrial powerhouse. Nor is there any indication that they wanted it to. They were quite comfortable with the original arrangement: a small clique of German saloon keepers had made a personalized kingdom they controlled with impunity. No one challenged their authority until those "damned Polacks" started moving in.

As early as December 1911, Hamtramck was already proclaimed "Detroit's Most Remarkable Suburb" by *Michigan Manufacturer* magazine, as major factories began moving into town. The magazine had a lot to base that on. Even before the Dodge plant opened, the village housed the sprawling Acme White Lead Paint Co., which opened in 1893. Following Dodge Main came a slew of other factories, mainly auto related, including Briggs Manufacturing, Swedish Crucible Steel Company, Champion Spark Plugs, American Radiator, Russell Wheel and Foundry, Detroit Carrier and Manufacturing Co., Michigan Smelting and Refining and Palmer-Bee, which manufactured conveyor belts for factories.

That was good for the town's revenue stream, but as the old political adage asserts, you can't always solve a problem by throwing money at it. The social issues raised by the exploding population were formidable. Many of the immigrants were poor, inadequately educated and unfamiliar with the ways of modern America. Children were sent to schools where

The Acme White Lead Paint Company, founded in 1893, was one of the factories that predated Dodge Main.

they couldn't understand what the teacher was saying. Their parents were in a similar situation as they tried to cope with the challenges of living in the big city. Most had lived on country farms in a land that had been decimated by its neighbors. In the nineteenth century, Poland had been conquered and divided by Austrians, Prussians and Russians. In essence, Poland as an independent nation had ceased to exist, although the language and culture survived surreptitiously and was transported to America by the immigrants. But so were the bad feelings ingrained in the immigrants. Trust in government was an absurd concept. But reliance on families for support could only accomplish so much, especially in a new land that resembled the old country in so many bad ways. The Germans and Poles were openly hostile in the Old Country. In Hamtramck, the hostility seemed to grow in proportion to the number of immigrants. Early arrivals after 1910 showed little interest in voting and had dismal turnout at the polls. They helped the German minority stay in power. Acts of voter suppression also helped with the imbalance of power. There are cases of the Hamtramck clerk's office closing voting polls at 4:00 p.m. on Election Day. Workers got off the job at 5:00 p.m. or later.

Pleas by the Poles for the clerk's office to hire a Polish-speaking person who could communicate with would-be voters were ignored.

But when the tidal wave heads directly toward you and there's no higher ground to flee to, the impact is inevitable. Around 1918, a rumor started circulating in town that the German saloon keepers were working on a deal with Detroit officials to allow Hamtramck to be annexed by Detroit but leave the saloon keepers in local control. There's no hard evidence that this was true, but it didn't matter back then. The Poles were outraged and formed the new Liberty Party, which was dedicated to the concept of having the village of Hamtramck incorporated as a city. There is a state procedure for cities to annex townships and villages, but the process is nearly impossible for a city to annex another city. By this time, the Poles had learned their political lessons and understood the power of the ballot.

Although all of the attention so far has focused on Polish and German people, it must be noted that they weren't the only people who lived in Hamtramck. Even before the Dodge invasion, small communities of Black people, Ukrainians, Russians and people of other nationalities lived in Hamtramck. In particular, Black people were pushed into the spotlight as the Germans and Poles vied for their support in the battle over cityship. The Poles won that battle, and ultimately, an election was held, and the vote favored becoming a city. Hamtramck did become a city in 1922. Soon, the German population faded to nearly nothing. The Black community briefly ascended to power, with the election of Ordine Toliver to the last village council in 1921 and Dr. James Henderson to the first city council in 1922. But by 1924—and continuing until the mid-1990s—virtually everyone elected to office was born in Poland or of Polish descent.

Hamtramck the city has been on a roller coaster ride since 1922, and it shows no sign of stopping even now. The city's population peaked at fifty-six thousand in 1930 and began an inevitable decline. There just isn't enough room to comfortably house fifty-six thousand people in 2.1 square miles, especially when there are no high-rise buildings in town. Further, standards of living had changed. In the early days, the Hamtramckans built cars; they didn't own them. Today, families have multiple cars but very few driveways and garages. Imagine how many cars would be jockeying for parking spots on a block where every house had as many as twenty occupants who owned who knows how many cars.

The population drifted downward through the 1930s and 1940s and really began to sink after World War II. At this point, the guys were coming home from the service. Some were already married and even had small children at home to greet them. Others were planning to wed, and often, it was the new bride who had her eyes on the attractions offered by the suburbs—big

Above: Ordine Toliver was the first Black man elected to public office in Hamtramck. That was in 1921. He later served as deputy city treasurer and held several prominent positions in city government. A man of many talents, he also was a music teacher.

Opposite: When the village of Hamtramck was formed in 1901, it was carved out of the much larger Hamtramck Township. The village borders remained almost unchanged when Hamtramck became a city in 1922, as reflected in this city map from 1939.

lawns, garages, driveways and modern amenities like bathroom showers, built-in ovens and enough electrical outlets to power every contraption in the house. So, the big exodus to the suburbs began, and the outlying communities like Warren (some call it Hamtramck North) underwent their own population explosions. Their gain was Hamtramck's loss. By 1990, the city's population stood at about eighteen thousand. While far lower than its peak number, it was not bad for a town of 2.1 square miles. No one was alarmed and neither did anyone seem to notice that the nature of the city was changing greatly. The Poles, who once made up 83 percent of the population, dwindled dramatically, eventually to under 10 percent. And more ethnic groups were arriving—Albanians, Chaldeans, Bosnians and, later, Yemenis and Bangladeshis, among many others. The trend continued into the twenty-first century. Hamtramck's 2000 census numbers showed the city's population at twenty-four thousand people, and the number has officially hovered there since. But there are those familiar with the city who would challenge that number as far too low.

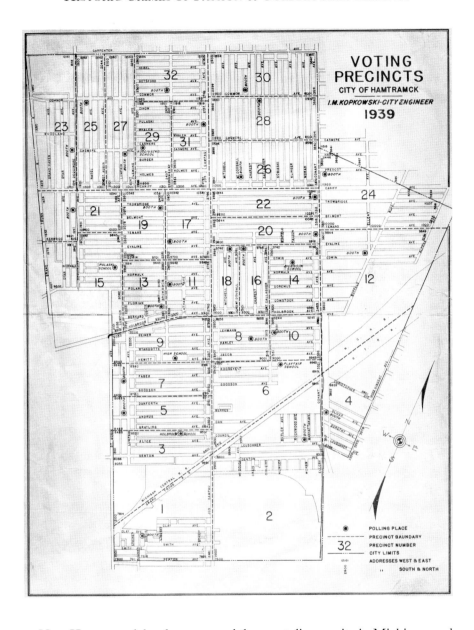

Now Hamtramck has been named the most diverse city in Michigan and one of the most diverse in the nation. That is reflected in that Hamtramck became the first town in America to elect a Muslim majority city council in 2015. And there is no indication that the trend toward more diversity won't continue.

So, those are killer statistics, but what has all this got to do with murder?

Hamtramck is a tapestry made of people, places and events that create an incredibly complex picture. In some way, these elements play a part in every murder that has occurred in the city. Consider that the city's legendary number of bars (at least two hundred at one time) made them likely targets of robbers, since there were so many in the labyrinth of city streets that a killer could disappear into. That proved fatally true for Peter Kubert, who was killed by Hamtramck's most notorious criminal, as you will see.

The Great Depression; persistent poverty; the issues that gambling creates; cramped living conditions; sexual tensions; the impact of Prohibition, which was overwhelming in Hamtramck; and more all played roles in the litany of murders. It almost seems as if every human flaw was magnified in the vast stage that was—and still is—Hamtramck. The converse was true, as well, as Hamtramck often brought out the most noble side of some. But their stories are for another time and place.

For now, we are going for a walk on the dark side.

2

EARLY MAYHEM

CASE NO. 1884-1

Homicide

Sunday, September 7, 1884, was supposed to be a day of joy for Fritz Krum, whose child was being christened. Instead, it ended with murder. A party later in the day at Krum's Hamtramck house stretched into the night, and it's likely that liquor flowed. In any case, trouble arose when a girl refused to dance with a party guest, Fritz Kerniffel. That led to a fight involving several people, including a man named Patrick Bourke. He was stabbed in the thigh, and the blade probably pierced an artery, as he quickly bled to death.

Brothers Charles and Herman Bartz, who were in the battle, blamed Kerniffel and another man, who, in turn, blamed the Bartz brothers. There's no record of who was charged.

CASE NO. 1885-1

Homicide

It seems natural to envision Hamtramck of the 1880s as a wilderness of forests and bogs. After all, there really wasn't much beyond the riverfront at that time. And it was less than thirty years since an eleven-year-old boy who was picking berries was eaten by a bear. But consider this opening line in a story that appeared in the August 13, 1869 edition of the *Detroit Post*: "A cloud of smoke hanging on the south-eastern portion of the city marks the iron manufacturing quarter of Hamtramck….The rise and development of manufacturing in Hamtramck are highly encouraging to the city. What has been accomplished shows just what may be accomplished, if activity and enterprise continue to characterize the management."

The story makes reference to the lousy air quality that accompanies the manufacturing success. In fact, it kind of revels in it. Recalling the recent past, the story notes, "Where were then orchards and green fields, stretching down to the pleasant bank of the river, are now docks, loaded down with coal and iron, warehouses filled with manufacturers, and furnaces and foundries whose smoke blackens the face of the sky, while below run streams of liquid fire, and swarms of grimy workmen in action here and there."

The Dodge Main factory (at left, behind the big smokestack) changed the character of Hamtramck, as it turned what was mainly farmland into a heavily industrial landscape in a matter of a few years. With that growth came urban problems, including homicide.

Charming. Also, this was a sign of prosperity. And then, like now, that was treasured more than "orchards and green fields" by some. And if you liked smoke and grime, there was indeed a lot to revel in. The Detroit Stove Works was actually in Hamtramck, located on Jefferson Avenue, where the Belle Isle Bridge is located today. Founded in 1861 by Jeremiah and James Dwyer and Thomas Mizer the factory was opened on the riverfront. By 1887, the plant had 1,300 employees and produced seven hundred types of stoves. By the end of the nineteenth century, stove making was Detroit's leading industry. And just to avoid confusion, the terms *Detroit* and *Hamtramck* in this context are interchangeable. They were distinct government entities with their own mayor (Detroit) and supervisor (Hamtramck) and city council and board of trustees, but they coexisted and commingled despite the technical borderlines.

And in both towns, there were many other types of businesses. Thomas Campau & Co. was typical. It specialized in "Groceries, Flour, Feed, etc." It stood at the corner of Iron Street and Jefferson Avenue just outside of Downtown Detroit, although it was in Hamtramck Township.

Business was one facet of Hamtramck Township. At the other end of the development spectrum was the Hamtramck Race Course. Its purpose was

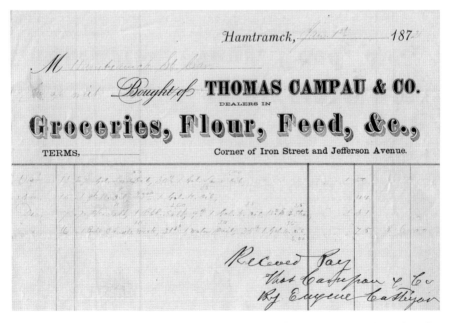

Thomas Campau & Co. near the riverfront was a typical Hamtramck Township business in the late nineteenth century. This receipt dates to 1872.

pleasure, nothing more. Located just north of Jefferson Avenue across from Belle Isle, the racecourse opened in 1853 (another source says 1843) and was pretty impressive, with large grandstands and a pavilion. By 1885, it was a popular gathering place and held other events, including an ill-fated staged buffalo hunt in 1862 that completely flopped when the buffaloes ignored the hunters and munched on the grass. There was no sport in shooting munching buffaloes, and "the spectators withdrew in disgust," according to a newspaper account.

The Hamtramck Race Course operated until about 1893, when it was superseded by another racecourse that opened in Grosse Pointe.

We have established that Hamtramck Township, by the 1880s, was a fairly developed community, at least along the area near the riverfront. So, the challenges of frontier life can't be used as an excuse for why Steven McEnally, age seventeen, stabbed his best friend to death in October 1885. Details are scarce, but it was reported that McEnally stabbed Burwell Sales in the heart after a night of drinking on Jefferson Avenue. McEnally also stabbed Frank Durah and seriously, perhaps fatally, injured him. There was no follow-up report.

McEnally was captured quickly after the crime when he was leaving his home where he had gone to wash the blood off his hands. Supposedly, Sales was a fine person, while McEnally was a "good-natured fellow when sober."

CASE 1908-1

Homicide

Annie Schultz sat quietly in the room waiting for the axe to fall. It did—several times—on the head of her husband. He was in his bedroom, where he had retired, never dreaming that this night would be his last. Delivering the axe blows was Annie's lover, John Kurka, who was the victim's half-brother, Anthony Schultz. Kurka lived in the same house as the Schultzes.

The motive was nothing new—Annie and John were in love. Anthony stood between them. At least he did until about 3:30 a.m. on Sunday, November 8, 1908, when Kurka crept into Anthony's bedroom and struck him in the head several times. Annie could hear every blow. After the murder was done, Kurka called Annie into the bedroom. Annie grabbed her husband by the feet, while Kurka lifted him by the shoulders. Together, they carried his body to a wagon waiting outside. Then, Kurka began a journey of several miles across Detroit and into the wilds of Hamtramck Township, where the body was dumped by the side of the road and covered with straw. And that is where it was found. It didn't take police long to trace the crime back to John Kurka, who quickly confessed.

Annie was brought in by police. Kurka was there. "Annie, I've told them all about it," he said. She began sobbing hysterically and fell into a chair, where she carried on for ten minutes as the police officers present quietly waited. She and Kurka were arraigned on a charge of murder before a Hamtramck justice of the peace, and the case was transferred to Wayne County court.

CASE No. 1909-1

Homicide

Move on, folks, just move on. There's nothing to see here—nothing except a woman, about age thirty-five, whose battered body was found. There was evidence of a frantic struggle. Whatever happened, she put up a fight. But that's all we know of this killing in August 1909.

Early Hamtramck Township clustered along the Detroit River. Much of the area was unsettled, although there were toll roads, as this three-dollar toll bill from 1876 shows. The isolated character made it popular for wayward drunks and occasional murders.

CASE NO. 1910-1

Homicide

If you lived in Hamtramck in 1910, chances are you would have heard of the Howcroft family. They had been in the newspapers several times, and the stories weren't always nice.

There had been some brushes with the law, and their quarreling was the subject of some discussion around town. As far back as 1908, the death of Mrs. Howcroft drew interest, when John Young, her son-in-law, reported to the newspapers that that the lady died after drinking carbolic acid following a family argument over money. Her sons, however, insisted that she died of natural causes, and "the sons say it's nobody's business what Mrs. Howcroft died of," said Justice Binder of Hamtramck. "Under the circumstances, I don't feel like taking responsibility of ordering an inquest. If, however, the citizens of the township demand it, I shall certainly inquire into the case thoroughly and get to the bottom of it. There have been some ugly rumors and I would not be surprised to receive a petition asking for an inquest. In that case I shall act quickly."

Justice Binder did not order an autopsy of the body, either, saying he would do so if the public demanded it, "but there's no hurry about that." A funeral was held in the Howcroft family home on Van Dyke Avenue, just north of Forest Lawn Cemetery, where Mrs. Howcroft was later buried. She was sixty-five years old when she died and left a large family. Along with her husband, Mark, she was survived by six sons, Will, George, Herbert, Samuel, Adam and Mark Jr., and six daughters, E. Watson, Polly Bellinger, Anna Osborn, Sarah Pickard, Harriet Blaess and Vina Young.

"For years a bitter feud has existed between the Howcrofts and the Blaesses, who are related by marriages and their jangles have brought them often into court," the *Detroit Times* noted.

At this time, there were two Hamtramck's: the village of Hamtramck and Hamtramck Township. The Township once covered a good section of the metropolitan Detroit area, stretching all the way to Lake St. Clair and the Detroit River. It shrank throughout the nineteenth century as Detroit grew and annexed it a bit at a time. Hamtramck village was itself carved out of the township in 1901 and became a separate community. In 1910, the area where the Howcrofts lived was still part of the township but would be absorbed by Detroit in 1916. Van Dyke Avenue remains a major Detroit street, and Forest Lawn Cemetery is also in operation today. The distinction between the village and township explains the presence of Justice Binder, who acted separately from the village of Hamtramck, which had its own administration and justice of the peace who held court in a small building on Jos. Campau Avenue near Miller Street.

It doesn't look as though there ever was an inquest into Mrs. Howcroft's death, but all this was a fitting prelude to what was going to happen next.

"Hamtramck Man Blows Son's Head off with Gun" was the not-too-subtle headline on the front page of the *Detroit Times* on August 22, 1910. "The bickerings of the Howcroft family has finally resulted in murder, the father, Mark, Sr., having killed his youngest son, Mark, Jr., 23 years old by blowing the top of his head off with a shotgun about 10 o'clock Sunday night," the story read.

He then fled the house with two guns, saying he was going to kill himself. But two hours later, Deputy Sheriff William Martz found Howcroft hiding at the house of his nephew George in Norris Village, which is centered on Mount Elliott and Nevada Streets, less than a mile northwest of the Howcroft farmhouse. Howcroft was arrested and taken to the Wayne County Jail.

Mark Howcroft lived in the farmhouse with two of his sons, Mark Jr. and Jack, and their wives, who were present at the time of the murder. According

The lonely remnants of the Norris house on Mount Elliott Street near Stockton Street just north of modern-day Hamtramck. Until it was nearly destroyed by a fire, this was the core of Norris Village, near where the Howcroft murder took place.

to their story, the father and son argued before the senior Howcroft fired, hitting his son in the head. It wasn't the first time Howcroft had a dispute with one of his sons. In the fall of 1909, Howcroft accused son Samuel of stealing $700 from a hiding place in the cellar of the farm. Samuel was arrested and charged with theft, but he was acquitted by a circuit court jury when it was shown that most of the money had been deposited in a bank.

After Howcroft shot Mark Jr., son Jack managed to wrestle the gun away from Howcroft, who then supposedly "fell over the corpse" of his son and cried, "Whatever in the world got into me to do this?" He then got up, gathered two other guns he had in the house, along with all the money he could pull together, and fled. The local sheriff was called and sent deputies Martz and Stein to find Howcroft. They searched the Howcroft farm but failed to locate him. But they got a tip that he might have gone to his nephew's place in Norris Village, so they headed over there. The nephew told them that Howcroft had been at the house but left and was planning to go to the county jail to give himself up. Just to be sure, the deputies searched the area and found Howcroft in the back, where he was getting into a buggy. They arrested him without incident.

In September 1910, Howcroft's preliminary examination was held. Among the witnesses called were county physician Dr. Edwin Forbes and coroner J.W. Rothacher. Forbes testified that death was caused by a fractured skull and injury to the brain consistent with a gunshot wound. He said the gunshot entered the forehead just above the left eye and blew away the front part of the head. There were powder burns on his face, and he believed the gun was about three to six feet away from Mark Jr. when fired.

By now, Mark Sr. had an attorney, Charles T. Wilkins, and Wilkins made it clear early on that he was going to push a case of self-defense. Wilkins got Forbes to say that the shot had been fired at an angle. Then, dramatically, he took the gun, rested the stock on the floor and held the barrel in his left hand. He asked Forbes if it was possible that the kind of wound Mark Jr. suffered could have been made from the gun being held in that position if he had stood three feet away and the gun fired at a slant. Forbes said it was possible. Dr. Rothacker was also questioned by Wilkins and corroborated what Dr. Forbes said, including the nature of the injuries. Wilkins jumped on it.

"Now if the shooting were done intentionally, and the gun were aimed at a man just a few feet away, would not the shot have entered direct and carried away the back portion of the head as well?" he asked.

"I believe it would," Dr. Rothacker said.

As ghastly as the case was, the press noted that, curiously, the bickering Howcroft family seemed to be coming together as one in defense of Mark Sr. At the examination, the wife of son Jack testified that Mark Jr. was his dad's favorite son and he would do things for him that he wouldn't for anyone else. She said she heard part of the scuffle that occurred on the night of the killing but wasn't in the room when the shot was fired. She testified, however, that Mark Sr. said, "My God, my boy, I didn't know the old gun was loaded." That was in contrast to the earlier assertion that he said, "Whatever in the world got into me to do this?"

In another fundamental shift, when son Jack took the stand, his testimony varied greatly from what he had told police after the shooting. Earlier, he said the father and son had fought frequently, and only a week prior to the fatal shooting, the father had threatened to kill his son. On the stand, he said he had no memory of the father ever making any threats. Supporting the approach that the shooting was accidental, he said that the gun used by Mark Sr. had exploded the day before, when he tried to shoot at a rat.

Mark Howcroft Sr. was bound over for trial, which took place in October 1911. He faced a charge of murder, but it was already clear that the prosecution was in for a major battle. The prosecutor's own witnesses were coming against him. Even Mark Howcroft Jr.'s wife took a stand with the other family members that the shooting was an accident. The frustration of the assistant prosecutor, named Aldrich, soon became evident as Mark's widow's frequent answer to questions were "I don't remember." Finally, there was the following exchange.

"You have talked this matter over with the other members of the family, haven't you?" he asked.

"We agreed to tell the truth," she said.

"You have repeated the story you were to tell several times with the other, haven't you?" he asked.

"We have talked about it, yes, and we said we would tell the truth," she said.

"As a matter of fact, hasn't the whole family met and agreed upon a story and decided to call it an accident," he asked.

At this point, Howcroft's attorney objected, saying he was trying to impeach his own witness.

"I'm not trying to impeach my own witness," Aldrich hurled back. "You will see what we are up against in this case, your honor. The only witnesses to the shooting were members of the family, and they have united in the defense of the prisoner."

The judge sided with defense attorney Wilkins. On further questioning, Mrs. Howcroft said her husband and father-in-law were not quarreling at the time of the shooting.

Faced with that kind of testimonial backtracking, it's almost a wonder that it took the jury twenty hours to come up with its verdict, which was no verdict. "We are split on the question of fact," jury foreman Sidney R. Miller told the judge when the jury marched into the court room at 9:40 a.m. on Friday, October 20, 1911. The issue was whether Mark Howcroft Sr. was pulling the gun forward to shoot his son or was pushing it backward when it accidentally fired.

The jury had been deliberating since 2:45 p.m. the previous afternoon, except when the members stepped out for a "big beef steak supper" at the upscale Normandie Hotel at 7:00 p.m. on Thursday. Although they deliberated all night, no progress was made. The jury was dismissed, but the case remained pending while the prosecutor decided if he wanted to try it again.

Mark Howcroft Sr. said he was disappointed with the outcome, as he had expected to be acquitted "within two minutes" after the jury began deliberations. He was accompanied by his daughter Sarah, who said, simply, "Father is innocent."

The jury had made a pact to not discuss the deliberations with anyone after the trial, but jury watchers said that judging by their faces the jury was hung up by two men. And that's where the matter rested.

CASE NO. 1915-1

Suspected Homicide

Hamtramck had barely gotten sewers in 1915, when the body of an infant girl was found in one behind a house on Moran Street in March of that year.

Plumbers doing work on the pipe discovered the body and called police chief Barney Whalen. County physician E.L. Brandt examined the body but was unable to determine if the infant had been alive when placed in the drain. Police questioned five people but learned nothing. This was a time when illegitimate pregnancies were a lot more common than people today think. And the stigma of being an unwed mother was far harsher than it is now. Perhaps the child had been stillborn, which would have made it more likely that the mother would have tried to hide it forever. But if the mother had a more sinister intent, the child's life had barely begun before it ended in a sewer. As for the mother, she likely carried this story to her own grave.

Case No. 1916-1

Double Homicide/Assault

By 1916, the village of Hamtramck had somewhere around twenty thousand residents and was growing. Although it was still a village, it was acquiring the aspects of a big city, including crime.

And a particularly horrific one occurred in December 1916 in a Hamtramck grocery and meat store. Lucy Martyniak, age five, shielded her brother while her father and grandfather were shot to death by three thieves. They also seriously wounded Lucy's mother, Agnes, who was shot in the side.

Joseph Martyniak and John Jaskolski died at the scene, and Agnes was transported to Samaritan Hospital. As with many of these early cases, details are scant, and whether the killers were caught is not known.

Case No. 1917-1

Multiple Homicides/Suicide

Warning: If you are squeamish or even just sensitive, skip this case, for this is the stuff that horror movies are made of.

"Hamtramck Mother Hangs Three Children and Self." That two-deck banner headline screamed across the top of the front page of the *Detroit Times* newspaper on Saturday, September 22, 1917. The mother was Julia Mikula, twenty-eight, who lived in the upper flat of a house at 2018 St. Aubin Street. She was married to John, who worked at the Enterprise Foundry on Warren Avenue in Detroit. They had four children: Olga, age three; June, age not given; Yolam, eighteen months; and John Jr., age nine. It was John Jr. who discovered June hanging from her bed post that Saturday afternoon. Horrified, he ran to the upstairs neighbor and told her what he had seen. However, she did not believe him and would not come downstairs to see. He returned to the first-floor flat and found his mother hanging from a chandelier. Even more shocked, John desperately ran back upstairs to the neighbor for help. This time, she believed him enough to come and see. She accompanied the boy downstairs, where more horror unfolded. Olga and Yolam were found hanging from clothes hooks in bedrooms at the front and back of the flat.

Neighbors called the police. They investigated and brought in the Wayne County coroner. No motive was found for the killings. There was no indication of family problems, and neighbors said they seemed like a fine couple living in a neatly kept, happy household. Ultimately, they concluded that Julia Mikula had simply gone insane.

CASE NO. 1917-2

Multiple Homicides

Hamtramck was once referred to at the Wild West of the Middle West, and from time to time, it really was. A prime case was the wild shootout that occurred at 11:00 p.m. on Monday, January 22, 1917, on Jos. Campau Avenue, Hamtramck's main street.

The perpetrator was Lee White, who had recently separated from his wife and was living at a house owned by Mr. and Mrs. Stephen Aston on Jacob Street, just east of Jos. Campau. White's friend and witness to what was to come Carl Vess told police that White said he wanted to reconcile with his wife and asked Vess to come with him to the Astons' house. The plan was to have Vess ring the doorbell while White stood behind in the shadows. Vess rang the bell, the door opened and White pushed his way inside, where he wife was. White immediately started shooting, and his wife ran out onto the street. Mrs. Aston came to the door and was shot by White, who then ran after his wife, shooting. The shots attracted Victor Kellner, who operated an electrical supply store at Jos. Campau Avenue and Jacob Street. Kellner got his gun and ran outside, where he saw White approaching. He warned White to stop, but was fatally shot by White before he could raise his own gun. But as Kellner fell to the street, he fired one shot, striking White in the back. Badly hurt, White managed to fire several more times, and one of the shots hit his wife in the back, mortally wounding her.

It was in this area of Jos. Campau Avenue that Victor Keller and Lee White engaged in their fatal gun battle.

Later, Vess confessed to police that the whole thing had been planned. He said that White had given him his valuables as if he was on a suicide mission. Vess said the original plan was to get into the Aston house, and when going out, he would leave the door open so that White could enter and kill his wife and the Astons. It didn't work out that way.

CASE NO. 1919-1

Homicide

On December 8, 1919, Hamtramck police put out a wanted poster that was spread nationally, offering $300 for the capture of Pol (Alias Paul) Teresko, who was wanted for the murder of Rose Solzsiak of 42 Dorothy Street. He had cut her throat with a razor.

Teresko, age thirty, was described as five feet, eleven inches and 220 pounds, with a sandy complexion.

"The man is a Russian and has been employed in auto factories," the poster noted.

The poster circulated at least as far as New York, but whether Teresko was caught is not known.

Bod.

$E484$

Hamtramck Police Department

Hamtramck, Mich., December 8th, 1919

$300.⁰⁰ REWARD!
Wanted for Murder

On December 4th, 1919, about 8:30 p. m., POL. alias PAUL TERESKO, age 30, 220 pounds, 5 ft. 11, sandy complexion, smooth face, went to 42 Dorothy street, Hamtramck, Mich., and killed Mrs. Rose Solzsiak by cutting her throat with a razor.

This man is a Russian and has been employed in auto factories.

We hold a warrant for this man's arrest. Address or wire all communications to

FRED B. DIBBLE

Chief of Police

Hamtramck, Michigan

This wanted poster made it all the way to New York, where it was found years later, as the search for murder suspect Paul Teresko went nationwide.

CASE No. 1921-1

Attempted Murder by Lynching

In many respects, Hamtramck was exceptionally progressive in the area of race relations. As previously mentioned, in 1921, a Black man, Ordine Toliver, was elected to the last Hamtramck village council just as the immigrant surge hit its peak and forced the village to hold an election and officially become a city. That happened in 1922, and with that, another Black man, Dr. James Henderson, was elected to the first Hamtramck Common Council. The Hamtramck public schools were fully integrated from their earliest years in the 1890s. And the Hamtramck Police Department was also integrated by the 1920s, when there were several Black police officers and detectives. In the 1920s, it was not unusual for Black people to own a home in Hamtramck, live on one floor and rent the other to White immigrant families. At that time, Black and White people living in the same house owned by Black people was virtually unheard of in the rest of the country.

So, perhaps it's not too surprising that Hamtramck police helped rescue a young Black man who was about to be lynched. The story played out in 1921, when lynching Black people was still common in the South.

Detroit police received a call about a riot breaking out at a baseball game at a local field. Hamtramck police were called in to assist and help rescue Sam Griggs, a Black youth, whose cousin Owen Griggs had struck a White kid in an argument over a seat at the game. Owen fled to his cousin Sam's house nearby, followed by an angry crowd. Sam Griggs came out to meet the crowd and was handed a gun by his sister, Mary Andrews. Sam fired into the crowd, wounding two twelve-year-old boys. The crowd attacked Sam, beating him with their fists and baseball bats. Someone brought a rope and placed a noose around Sam's neck, proclaiming that they were going to lynch him.

That's when Hamtramck police officer Stanley Goralczyk arrived and attempted to rescue Sam. Goralczyk was also attacked and beaten, but more officers arrived and managed to rescue Sam and Officer Goralczyk and break up the crowd. Sam admitted to the shooting but said he was fired at first. Sam, Owen and Mary Andrews were all arrested, but no one was killed.

3

JUST DON'T DRINK

For many people in Hamtramck, the years 1919 to 1933 (in Michigan) marked the new Dark Ages. The rest of the country called it Prohibition.

It's not that Prohibition posed any particular constraints on the quality of life then. It is true that the production and sale of alcohol was forbidden, but that meant virtually nothing to Hamtramckans. In fact, for many Hamtramck residents, Prohibition was an opportunity that helped bring balance to the Great Depression, which coincided with the last few years of Prohibition. Maybe there were no more jobs at the factory, but you could be self-employed making beer and stronger booze in the attic or shed out back. If you didn't get caught and thrown in jail, you could make at least a few bucks to help keep the family afloat. No one knows how many speakeasies—and their cousins, the blind pigs and brothels—operated in Hamtramck during the Prohibition years, but surely, the number was in the hundreds. And that doesn't take into account the vast array of illegal stills that are still found to this day stashed between walls and in the back of basements.

Hamtramck was in a unique position during Prohibition. As an independent town completely surrounded by Detroit and only five miles from the Detroit River, it was somewhat like Switzerland during World War II. It was neutral ground amid hostile forces. Liquor was easily smuggled across the Detroit River from Canada, where it could be hauled to the speakeasies in Hamtramck. Detroit had its own speakeasies that numbered in the thousands, but what made Hamtramck special is that the Detroit cops had no pull there. So, if a Detroit politician or priest or person of the

Police examine an illegal still. These were common during the Prohibition era, when seemingly everyone was making booze in their basement or attic or garage or wherever.

press wanted to find a soft seat to drink in peace without being bothered by anyone, Hamtramck was the place to go. That's not to say that Hamtramck didn't have its own share of bad actors. Chester LaMare was in the major leagues of organized crime. His spaghetti restaurant, the Venice Café, on Jos. Campau north of Caniff Avenue was a notorious trouble spot. That didn't stop Hamtramck's first mayor, Peter Jezewski, from being a regular visitor, even against the advice of fellow politicians.

Jezewski ignored his cronies and got involved in bootlegging, eventually ending up in Jackson Prison for his efforts. And he wasn't the only mayor to do time in the big house. Dr. Rudolph Tenerowicz served two terms as mayor and a stretch in prison for Prohibition violations. His supporters were horrified. No, not because he broke the law but because the government had the audacity to throw him in the slammer when he got caught. In response to that indignity, thousands of Hamtramckans signed a petition claiming Doc Ten, as he was called, was railroaded and should be set free. At that point,

Right: Peter Jezewski was elected as Hamtramck's first mayor when the village incorporated as a city in 1922. He quickly ran afoul of the law when Prohibition was enacted, and he served a stint in prison. That contributed to Hamtramck's reputation as the Wild West of the Midwest.

Below: Mayor Rudolph Tenerowicz was an exceptionally popular mayor. Even though he was sent to prison for a Prohibition violation, he was later elected to Congress.

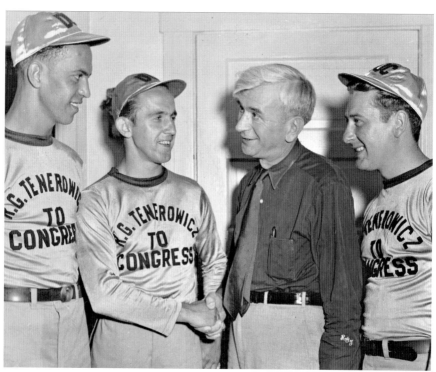

in 1934, William Comstock, a Democrat, was governor. He received the petition and did the political math. Hamtramck had a population of about fifty-six thousand people, and they voted overwhelming for Democrats. And they all voted. It wasn't unusual for an election to draw more than 90 percent voter turnout.

Tenerowicz was pardoned.

And then he was elected to Congress.

But years before the Tenerowicz incident, Hamtramck was already recognized as a hot spot of corruption. In 1923, the state police came into Hamtramck to take over police operations. In six months, they had raided dozens of speakeasies and places with illegal stills. On some blocks, such as Mitchell Street north of Holbrook Avenue, as many as six houses in a row were raided. But often the state police would arrive to find that their prey had vanished, tipped off by the Hamtramck cops who were on the take. Eventually, the exasperated state police basically gave up, declared victory and left town. The mess really wouldn't be cleaned up until well after Prohibition ended and the housewives in town got fed up with the endless drinking and hookers on the porches of the whorehouses attempting to entice even their children. They literally beat the law breakers out of town with broomsticks.

But while it lasted, Hamtramck was one wicked place. Yet, oddly, the murder rate didn't seem to skyrocket during Prohibition. Crime did flourish, especially in areas like the juvenile delinquency rate, which posed a particular problem. Interestingly, Mayor Tenerowicz, out of prison, joined forces with legendary tennis coach Jean Hoxie to develop a broader tennis program to draw vulnerable youths away from crime and into sports. But the juvenile delinquency problem persisted well beyond Prohibition and into the 1930s.

There were numerous gangs of adults who carved out their own territory, as often shown in their names, like the Hanley (Street), the Grand Haven, the Moran and the Leucshner gangs. But there was no St. Valentine's Day—or perhaps more appropriately something like a St. Gorazdowski's Day—massacre in Hamtramck. The mobsters seemed to keep their distance from each other. That's not to say there weren't some shocking moments in Hamtramck during this lively time. For instance, Mitchell Watchowski, forty-seven, of Dequindre Street had a fatal run-in with a group of boys, but the case might not be as clear-cut as it first seems.

Watchowski was attending a wedding at American Legion Hall at Leuschner and Denton Streets, where he stepped outside, possibly just to get some fresh air. There he encountered a group of boys across the street making a lot of noise. He told them to leave, but they refused to move.

Left: Necessity promotes creativity. What better way was there to transport illegal liquor than in the false bottom on an innocent-looking baby carriage.

Below: During Prohibition and the Great Depression, gangs became common. It's interesting to note that this gang was integrated.

Watchowski grabbed a board lying nearby and swung it at them. One of the boys knocked the board from Watchowski's hands, causing him to fall and hit his head on a railing on the sidewalk. He was taken to St. Francis Hospital, where he died a week later of a fractured skull. He regained consciousness once but was unable to make a statement.

The boys were questioned by police, but there wasn't evidence to prove they were responsible for his death.

PROHIBITION CASE-1

Homicide

About all we can say for certain about the death of Barney Roth is that he was one of a handful of police officers who were murdered. In most cases, the circumstances were straight forward. In Roth's case, the facts changed almost as soon as they were revealed.

At about 8:00 a.m. on Saturday, July 5, 1930, Roth was sitting in the kitchen of his house on Mitchell Street eating breakfast when two men entered through the back door and shot him. Barney's wife, Annette, was in the bedroom dressing their daughter Violet and later told police that she heard Barney say to someone, "I can't do anything for you. I told you that before." She then heard shots. She raced out of the bedroom still holding Violet, and one of the men grabbed her by the arms and pushed her back into the bedroom. She said he then fired two shots at her but missed.

The other gunman said to the first, "Don't shoot her" and shot Barney again. They both ran out of the house and escaped in a car.

Annette told police that she recognized one of the men who had come by three weeks earlier to get Barney's help with some case. He refused. And ten days before the shooting, another man had come to the house and told Barney that if he didn't help their house would be bombed. Again, he refused.

The killing of Barney Roth drew national attention. The next day, the *Evening Star* newspaper of Washington, D.C., reported the killing under the headline "Two Are Murdered in Detroit." The second man was identified as Johnny Metz, who had been sitting on the front porch of the Roths' house waiting for Barney to take him to federal court, where he was going to be arraigned for bootlegging. Roth had agreed to help Metz, Annette said. Metz heard the shots and ran inside the house, where one of the gunmen shot him.

The official police report on
the murder of Barney Roth
indicating that he had been shot
with a .45-caliber gun.

Barnard J. Roth had joined the Hamtramck police force on February 1,
1924, and was assigned to a plain clothes division to enforce Prohibition laws.
At that time, the Hamtramck Police Department was rife with corruption,
as speakeasies abounded, and illegal liquor production was common all over
town. Grand juries and outside law enforcement had little success in curbing
the flow of liquor. State police officers were routinely thwarted by local
police, who were on the take from the bootleggers and gangsters.

No one accused Roth of corruption, but it was obvious that the bootleggers
were putting pressure on him for some form of help.

In August 1930, the state police raided the Grosse Pointe Farms home
of Joe Catalanotte, a gangster who was associated with the gang of Chester
LaMare, who was known as the "Vice King of Hamtramck." LaMare ran
a fierce and fearless operation. At one point, a Hamtramck police officer,
embolden by the very drink he was supposed to eliminate, burst into LaMare's
restaurant with plans to arrest him. LaMare's men took the officer's gun,
beat him and dumped him at the front desk of the police station.

The state police arrested Catalanotte, along with Elma Macklin, and
charged them with murdering Roth. But the trial proved fruitless. Witnesses

Kegs of beer and bottles of gin weren't the only targets of police. Gambling devices like these slot machines were chopped to bits.

failed to show up or would not identify the shooters, and even Mrs. Roth changed her story, stating that she was in the bedroom changing Violet when she heard the shots and her husband scream. After waiting for a moment, she said, she rushed into the dining room, where she found her husband, but the shooters had gone.

The killers were never caught.

What happened? No one knows for sure. But after an investigation was done, the word was that Roth had been working with the mobsters and had betrayed them to the police.

The whole incident is reflective of the times. Law and order were so thoroughly demolished in Hamtramck that armed killers murdered a police officer in his home on a Saturday morning, seemingly with no fear of repercussions. Granted, almost the entire population of the city hated Prohibition, but the coldblooded killing of Barney Roth was not the same as sneaking a beer in a back room. And it certainly appears that his killers acted with impunity, confident that they could kill anyone who did not do as they wanted. Once a system is that broken, fixing it can be extremely difficult, as we will see.

There is a curious footnote to this story. In 1936, the incident was resurrected when it was learned that the child held by Annette on that bloody Saturday was not Roth's child. Annette was actually Annette Valquette, who was an unwed mother from Montreal, Canada, who came to the United States illegally and posed as Roth's wife, although they were never married.

This was of special interest to the city because the child was receiving a forty-dollar-a-month pension under the assumption she was Roth's daughter. Annette was arrested in January 1936 and was held in the county jail for several months before being deported.

Roth was not the only police officer to die under dubious circumstances. In September 1937, Hamtramck police detective John Page was fatally slashed with a razor when he attempted to break up a fight between Frazier Edwards and Buddy Walter, who were arguing over a fifty-cent bet in a gambling house on Russell Street in Detroit.

Page was not on duty at the time, and Edwards pleaded guilty to a manslaughter charge.

But what was Detective Page doing in an illegal gambling house in the first place?

PROHIBITION CASE-2

Homicide

The death of John Rusin was a classic Prohibition tale. Rusin was a successful bootlegger who liked to gamble. On January 7, 1930, he was trying his luck at a dice game in a blind pig at 7621 Jos. Campau Avenue, right by the railroad tracks just north of the Dodge factory. During the game, he got into an argument with Tommy Stapleton, who was a bartender at the blind pig. Bottom line: Stapleton shot Rusin through the heart and then disappeared. Shortly afterward, Rusin's body was found in an alley near the blind pig.

Skip ahead nearly four years to December 1933 in Miami, Florida. Police there had arrested a young man for vagrancy. While he was serving a ten-day sentence in jail, someone noticed that he looked like a man on a wanted poster being sought for murder in Hamtramck, Michigan.

Hamtramck detective sergeant Max Palucinski and an assistant prosecutor were sent to Miami to bring him back to Hamtramck, where he was arraigned before Judge Arthur Rooks in Hamtramck Court.

4

THE BLOODTHIRSTY '30s

The 1930s dawned in Hamtramck with the promise of a pending disaster. The stock market had just collapsed a few months earlier, and while few Hamtramckans owned stock, they worked for companies that sold them to help maintain their viability. And they got badly hurt—especially the car companies. Car sales fell dramatically—from 4.3 million units to 2.1 million from 1929 to 1932. The impact on Hamtramck was devastating. There were twenty-three factories operating in Hamtramck in 1929, and almost all were related to the auto industry. That included the gigantic Dodge factory, which was well on its way to becoming one of the biggest manufacturing plants in the world, until the Great Depression nearly ground its wheels of production to a halt. Soon, workers were being laid off. But where could they turn to for help?

In 1934, then mayor Joseph Lewandowski came up with the idea of having local factories commit to hiring unemployed Hamtramckans. The idea was to have at least one member of each family hold a job in one of the factories. Lewandowski even started to create a registration listing of all unemployed Hamtramckans. Nice idea. The problem was that there were no jobs at the factory to offer, so the plan failed.

That left many people turning to the city for public assistance. But the city almost instantly became overwhelmed, and the officials put in a requirement that a family had to have at least two children to qualify for assistance, as meager as it was.

Police commissioner Louis Wojcik (*left*) and Mayor Rudolph Tenerowicz try to brighten Christmas for a needy child during the Great Depression. Doesn't look like they are having much luck.

People also turned to the church for aid. St. Florian, Our Lady Queen of Apostles and St. Ladislaus Catholic Churches, as well as Corinthian and St. Peter AME, were the big churches, but even they couldn't do much to help. They relied on weekly donations from parishioners to operate. But in the depths of the Great Depression, those who could give anything at all to the church could barely manage more than a few pennies.

Dodge Main wasn't the only huge factory in Hamtramck. The Briggs plant nearby was an industrial powerhouse. Only a few years earlier, this area was farmland.

Social organizations also did what they could. Groups like the Tau Beta Community House and St. Anne's Community House assisted, but the need far outweighed the ability to help. People went hungry. Children went to school in raggedy clothes and shoes that fell apart if they went to school at all. People couldn't pay rent or make mortgage payments and lost their homes. Stacks of furniture piled on the curb became a frequent sight. Out of desperation, some families squatted in the city's voting booths, which were placed on various street corners during Election Day. The buildings were no more than a dozen square feet and were poorly constructed and heated by a lonely potbelly stove. Yet in desperation, families of squatters would find shelter there. Between elections, the voting shacks were stored at a lot behind Keyworth Stadium, and some people took up residence in them there.

The circumstances put people under unrelenting, grinding pressure. Some couldn't endure. The old newspapers are filled with accounts of people who hanged themselves in the attic, shot themselves in the barn out back or stepped in front of a moving train on one of the many sets of railroad tracks that nearly ringed the city.

St. Anne's Community House stood as a line of defense against the vice and corruption that were becoming prevalent in Hamtramck during Prohibition and the Great Depression.

In some respects, the young people were the most vulnerable but seemingly the most resourceful. With parents scrambling to make a living, they would often fend for themselves. There were few playgrounds in Hamtramck during the Depression. But the alleys had much to offer besides rats, trash and lines of decaying wooden barns that turned each alley into an urban canyon. They were places to play, to hunt rats (a once-popular

Living in Hamtramck could be challenging for a number of reasons during the early part of the twentieth century. Houses were built within a few feet of major factories. Noise, smoke and traffic put a strain on residents who tried to lead life ignoring those difficulties.

sport for urban kids), to smoke forbidden cigarettes and drink stolen alcohol. They were also good thoroughfares for more nefarious activity, like hauling stolen goods unseen. That became more of a concern with each passing year of the 1930s, as youth gangs began to prosper. Juvenile delinquency became a serious concern in the Depression years. It had a natural link to Prohibition, when Hamtramck became a virtually lawless town. In that period, however, the focus was on mainly the adult gangsters and the outfits like the Purple Gang, who were major-league bad boys ready to murder at the slightest provocation. The younger gang members could sometimes be almost comical in their exploits and naivety, but they were always just one bad move away from tragedy, either to themselves or others. Consider the Black Ace Gang. It consisted of John Poplowski, seventeen, of 2037 Belmont Street; Edward Lukaszewski, twenty-one, of 2241 Bernard Street; and Mike Pozniak, eighteen, of 2949 Belmont Street. In the spring and summer of 1936, these three pals robbed around two dozen houses in Hamtramck. And they weren't picky. They took what they could get, including an accordion worth $385, three guns, assorted jewelry and cash, cameras and even a pair of handcuffs from the house of a police officer.

But successfully stealing wasn't good enough. Inspired by the cheesy mystery movies they would watch at the local theaters (*Charlie Chan*, *Mr. Moto* and maybe the upscale *Thin Man* movies), they got the idea to send their victims a black ace of spades playing card with a personalized message like, "Next time keep your door closed. Remember your .32 gun?" "Don't be afraid. I only visit once, you poor sap" and "Too bad you didn't have more money because it would have come in handy right now. So how about going out sometime again and leaving a few hundred dollars—Black Ace."

And like in the movies, the cops were stumped until they got a big break. One day in August 1936, they got a call from the police in Bad Axe, a city in Michigan's "thumb," who said they had picked up Lukaszewski and Poplowski. Hamtramck detectives Joseph Kalinowski and Homer Ficht spent a good part of a Saturday going to Bad Axe—101 miles north of Hamtramck—and interviewing the boys. In the process, the cops went through their things and found a black ace of spades. The boys cracked. Pozniak was dragged into it, and they were eventually sentenced to two to five years in prison.

Pozniak's father said his son turned to crime because he (the father) had been out of work for a long time and couldn't afford to give his son any money. "All my family gets is a small welfare check," he said. As for the ace of spades bit, Poplowski's sister Jean said, "John is young, only 17, and something he saw in a movie probably stayed in his mind." But at least no one was killed. That wasn't always the case.

CASE 1930-1

Homicide

On the night of July 23, 1930, Jerry Buckley was in the lobby of the LaSalle Hotel on Woodward Avenue at Adelaide Street near downtown Detroit when he was approached by three men who shot him eleven times. It was a shockingly brazen murder, especially because Buckley was a popular radio commentator who had just led a successful effort to have corrupt Detroit mayor Charles Bowles recalled from office. Thousands of people turned out for Buckley's funeral, and the speculation, of course, was that the murder was retribution for the recall effort. Eventually, three men were brought to trial: Ted Pizzano, Joe Bommorito and Angelo Livechi.

During the course of the trial, the defense took a different approach in strategy. Defense attorney Anthony Maiullo announced that Buckley was not killed by gangsters associated with Mayor Bowles but rather by corrupt politicians associated with Hamtramck. His proof? The night Buckley was shot he was attending a party in the LaSalle Hotel, which was being thrown by a Hamtramck politician named William Janiszewski and attended by a group of Hamtramckans. Buckley was shot minutes after he left the party and had some association with Janiszewski. The people at the party learned quickly that Buckley had been assassinated but did not go down to the lobby for fifteen to twenty minutes and did not mention the party to any of the police present. The radio station that Buckley broadcast on was also located in the hotel, so there was no reason to question why he was at the hotel. But the defense even threw in the fact that the rooms where the party was held faced Adelaide Street, which is where the killers entered the hotel, perhaps signaled that the time was right by someone inside.

The lawyers weren't the first ones to try to tie Buckley to racketeers. After he had been murdered, the Detroit police commissioner charged that Buckley had taken a bribe from a bootlegger. Michigan governor Fred Green had the state police investigate the Detroit Police Department.

Ultimately, the defense did succeed. Later, Livechi and Pizzano were convicted of another murder. Three different men were identified as Buckly's killers but, ultimately, no one was ever convicted of the crime. As for Janiszewski, he never achieved any position of note in Hamtramck.

CASE NO. 1932-1

Homicide

There's no way to make sense of the death of seven-year-old John Chomacki. His body was found on Saturday, May 15, 1932, stuffed into a baby carriage inside a crumbling shack behind a house on Evaline Street.

He had been strangled with a chain. His mother, Emily Chomacki, earlier in the day became alarmed when he disappeared. She called police and John's uncle Frank Jackimovicz began his own search of the area. John did not have a father. His mother was a widow. It was the uncle who found John's body. Police pored through the area looking for clues. They theorized that John had been killed in the garage behind his home, across the alley from the shack from where his body was found. Police said John was last seen entering the garage behind his home and believed that the killer was waiting for him. Or perhaps he surprised the killer inside the garage. In fact, it turned out that his uncle was the killer. He acted with a friend to end the boy's life after John had seen the two involved in some criminal activity and he threatened to tell his mother.

Jackimovicz was sentenced to a long prison term.

CASE NO. 1934-2

Homicide/Robbery/Voodoo (Maybe)

Anyone can be the victim of a murderer. Even a voodoo priest.

Alex Jaffer was such a figure, but that didn't protect him from two young couples who robbed and murdered him in October 1934. Jaffer's landlady found him dead in his apartment at 2318 Norwalk Street. Neighbors told police that two young men and women were seen rushing out of the house.

Hamtramck detectives were able to identify the girls and arrested Margaret Skowron and Irene Wisniewski. They said that had been at Jaffer's apartment that night and implicated two young men, Sam Girodano, nineteen, and Dominic Brooklier, twenty. They were located, arrested and charged with murder and robbery, which they said was the motive for the killing. Jaffer usually wore a money belt, which could not be found. Both men denied knowing anything of the murder.

But almost as if he was under a curse, Giordano stood up at the trial and proclaimed his guilt. He said that he had strangled Jaffer after Jaffer had made advances on Skowron. However, he did deny robbing Jaffer. And he told police he didn't realize he had killed Jaffer until they told him he was dead.

In light of the confession, Brooklier was acquitted by the jury on a directed verdict.

CASE NO. 1934-3

Homicide

Frank Zajkowski was standing in front of a popular Detroit bar at Woodward Avenue and Baltimore Street at 2:00 a.m. on Sunday, May 3, 1942 (yes, 1942), talking with two other guys when one of them pulled a gun and shot him three times. Just like that. The two men then escaped in a car. It had all the markings of a mob hit and might have been—or maybe not. We will never know, even though Zajkowski lived for five hours before dying at Detroit Receiving Hospital. He could have made a statement to police but refused to say anything. That ended a long career of crime that included forty-seven arrests between 1923 and his death. Among that impressive list was one for the murder of Anthony J. Grossman, a Hamtramck underworld figure, way back in 1934. Zajkowski was identified as the killer and was the subject of an extensive manhunt. Even by then, he had a reputation as a gambler and drug addict.

The killing occurred on January 5, 1934, in the South End Club, at 2287 Newton Avenue, at the far southwest side of the city. There, Grossman was shot by his "friend" and South End Club bartender Thomas Bradley. And that was just the start of this strange tale. After shooting Grossman, Bradley called Frank Kew and Angelo Semino, two handymen who worked at the club, and had them carry Grossman's body to his car. But that's as far as they would go toward being accessories, so Bradley got into the driver's seat, with Grossman's body propped up in the seat to look like a live passenger.

"I was rattled and all I could think of was getting Tony's body away from the place," Bradley told police after he spent ten days in jail following his arrest in connection with the disappearance of Grossman. Not knowing where to go, he drove haphazardly north to Utica, Mount Clemens and finally New Baltimore, about thirty-five miles northeast of Hamtramck. Along the way, he drove up and down isolated side roads looking for a spot where there were no houses. Finally, he dumped Grossman's body in a culvert under Sugarbush Road, where it was found on January 21.

At first, police thought Bradley had solicited undertakers to store the body, as it was in such fresh condition when it was found. But it had just been preserved in the open by the January cold. When Bradley broke under police questioning, he led Prosecutor's Office investigators on a ride following his course, leading them to Grossman's body. Bradley claimed that he was in another room when Grossman was shot during a dice game. Enter Zajkowski. Three witnesses told police that Zajkowski came into the room and fired at Grossman without warning. As one of the witnesses fled the café, he told Grossman of the shooting. Grossman said he saw Zajkowski also fleeing from the place. Supposedly, Zajkowski shot Grossman for having thrown a friend of his out of the café earlier when he paid too much attention to a woman. While police began what would become a nationwide search for Zajkowski, Bradley was also charged.

"We can prove that Bradley was just as guilty as Zajkowski, and had a good reason to see Grossman killed," said Wayne County prosecutor Duncan C. McCrea. It took a year for police to track down Zajkowski, and when they did, Zajkowski beat the rap. He was acquitted in a trial marked by accusations of witness intimidation.

Zajkowski left Detroit but retuned a year before he was killed. Considering the company he kept, his demise was not surprising—nor was the fact that the killer was never found.

Case No. 1935-1

Homicide

Sometimes you just don't know what to say. Take the case of Valentine Pluta of 7732 Dubois Avenue. On September 29, 1935, he was arrested on suspicion of murder after police found the body of his roommate, Karol Klepatski, forty-eight, lying in bed with a bloodstained hammer at his side.

Police had been called to the address, and when they arrived, they found Pluta, forty-five, cooking a meal. A search of the residence led to Klepatski's body. Pluta was arrested and questioned by police. But there was nothing that could actually tie him to the murder. He was released the following day with instructions to appear at the police station if called. There's no record of him being called.

Case No. 1935-2

Homicide/Suicide

Welfare aid has always been a somewhat controversial and even emotional issue. That was especially true during the Great Depression, when welfare resources were scant and stressed. But in March 1935, the issue turned deadly.

Felix Fila of 12031 Nagel Street got into an argument with his next-door neighbor Andrew Wos. Fila contended that Wos reported him to the welfare department for receiving aid that he did not need. The argument turned deadly when Fila pulled a gun and shot Wos in the chest, arm and hand. Fila fled and hid in the home of a friend on nearby Dequindre Street. It was there that another chapter was added to the tragedy, as Fala shot himself. He was taken to St. Francis Hospital, where he died, leaving two daughters, ages fifteen and twelve, without a father.

CASE NO. 1936-1

Armed Robbery/Attempted Murder

A gun failed to fire when William Kryczkowski, eighteen, of Grayling Avenue pulled the trigger. That prevented Harry Pries of Detroit from being killed and Kryczkowski from being charged with murder.

But Kryczkowski was charged with armed robbery, as were his three companions, John Kowal, twenty-one, of Playfair (now Roosevelt Street); Stanley Plewinski, twenty, of Hanley Street; and Edward Tofil, twenty, of Lehman Street.

Circumstances of what exactly happened are a bit murky, but at 2:30 a.m. on August 28, 1936, Pries picked up the four youths at Michigan Avenue and Miller Street in Dearborn and drove them to Edwin Street at Alpena Street, where the four forced him out of his car and beat him.

Pries said that Kryczkowski pulled out a gun and pointed it at him and fired. But the gun apparently jammed. Kryczkowski said the gun was not aimed at Pries, and he was only trying to scare him.

Pries said the four stole his car, along with $31 in cash and a wire solder worth between $400 and $500. The youths said they only got $2 and that they didn't beat up Pries but only slapped him.

All four of the young robbers had extensive police records. Plewinski wasn't charged with armed robbery like the others. He had been paroled less than a month earlier from Jackson Prison and was immediately sent back for violating parole.

CASE NO. 1937-1

The murder of Bernice Onisko had a profound impact on the people of Hamtramck. To this day, her death in 1937 remains the most devastating murder in the city's history. The story began to unfold in the early morning of Sunday, March 7, when Bernice Kowalczyk went out to the back of her house bordering the alley at 12131 Botsford Street at the far north side of town. There she found the body of Bernice Onisko, who lived in a house nearby. She was lying on the ground, partially nude. Her scarf had been wrapped around her mouth, apparently to stifle her cries, and her belt was wrapped around her neck. She had been strangled.

Bernice Onisko's murder in 1937 shocked Hamtramck like none other before or since.

Onisko was known as a quiet, pious girl who did not appear to have any problems with her family. At 7:15 p.m. on Saturday, she went to St. Ladislaus Church eight blocks south of her house, where she was part of a mission. She had gone to church with her eleven-year-old sister, Loretta. Pastor Anthony Majewski later told police that he remembered seeing her siting alone in the church. A parishioner, Edward Trojnarski, said he saw Bernice leave the church when services ended at 8:55 p.m. and walk up Mackay Street toward her house with another girl. That person left her at Zinow Street, two blocks from Bernice's house. Police believe she was grabbed by her assailant, who pulled her in the alley where he raped her and strangled her with her belt. The killer had stuffed her scarf deep into her throat to silence her.

Her hat was found just inside the alley. Thirty-five feet farther into the alley, her shoe was found. Nearby her body was between two sheds. She weighed less than one hundred pounds and could hardly have put up a fight against her attacker.

The circumstances of her death shocked the community. Immediately, police began what has been probably the largest, longest investigation in Hamtramck police history. Within days of her death, police had nearly a dozen suspects and had arrested one. He was identified as a suspect by a shoeshine boy who had his stand at Jos. Campau and Caniff Streets, next to St. Ladislaus Church. The boy told police of a man who came to his stand on Saturday evening. What made him stand out was his unusually muddy shoes. The shoeshine boy was able to identify the man, and he was quickly arrested. But a daylong questioning session produced nothing and neither did a lie detector test administered to Onisko's cousin Onufry Zielinski, eighteen, who lived in the flat above the Oniskos on Niebel Street.

Almost immediately, and from this point on, the investigation started taking unusual, uncontrollable twists that pushed the police to the point of exasperation, especially since the investigation and lack of progress made front-page news for months. On Tuesday, following the murder, Bernice's mother, Cecilia Onisko, received a note "handwritten in pencil on cheap ruled note paper and mailed in a small linen-finished envelope" mailed from Detroit,

Bernice Kowalczyk indicates the area where she found the body of Bernice Onisko in an alley near her home.

according a to a newspaper account. It said, "Yes, I did it, but only after she bite [*sic*] my face and two fingers—she was like a tiger. When you get this I will be out of the state. What can I say more. What can I say—just amen."

That was it. There was no indication of who the writer was. A fingerprint was lifted from the note but could not be linked to anyone.

"We have had so many misfortunes," Bernice's mother told the press. "Peter, Bernice's father, died last July after he had been paralyzed a long time. Five years. I have been sick ever since, and we have had only my mother's pension to live on.

"Bernice was so little and thin. She was pretty though, with her blue eyes and light hair. But when she was 5 years old she was hit in the face with a baseball. It broke her nose. Sher had an operation, but for a long time lately her nose kept hurting her again, and she was to have another operation next."

She said Bernice had cleaned the house on the day of the murder and then made dinner. She went to church to pray for her mother's health and for a successful operation the next week. And she prayed to get a job. She had just graduated from St. Ladislaus School and was a good typist.

"She was such a smart girl," Mrs. Onisko said. "She never had a boyfriend, she never went out at night. She was a home girl and a church girl."

All these factors played into the public outrage that grew daily as her murder went unsolved. Seven police detectives and patrolman were assigned to the case but made no progress. To help nudge things forward, the Common Council offered a $500 reward "to speed up the capture." The council had considered a $1,000 reward but reduced it to $500, which was more in line with what the city could afford.

But, said Councilman Fred Dibble, the capture "was worth a million." Still, it didn't produce a dime's worth of progress.

Onisko's funeral was held at St. Ladislaus Church a week after her murder. It was one of the largest funerals in Hamtramck history. Thousands of people clustered around the Onisko house, where her body lay. A huge funeral procession followed her body to St. Ladislaus Church, where thousands more were gathered.

Within two weeks, some fifty people had been interviewed by Hamtramck police, and more were questioned by Detroit police. But after checking alibis, all were released. A handwriting expert was brought in to compare signatures of every city voter under age twenty-seven with the writing on the "confession" note Bernice's mother had received to see if there was a match. There wasn't. But there was a heightened awareness of sex crimes in the community. Two weeks after the Onisko murder, two sex crimes were reported to police. One involved a seven-year-old boy who was lured into an alley by a man who promised him candy and took off his clothes. But the man was scared away by a passerby before anything worse happened. In the other case, a man broke into the house of a woman and attempted to attack her in bed, where she lay sick. An upstairs neighbor was alerted and scared the man away.

On March 25, police detective captain John Sikorski reported that another dozen potential suspects had been questioned, but no progress had been made in the case. In time, the story drifted off the front pages of the newspapers, but it remained in the background like a dark cloud on the horizon. It was even pulled into a totally unrelated issue when *Newsweek* magazine did an exposé on the rampant corruption in Hamtramck at the time. The article outraged many Hamtramckans and prompted the Polish Roman Catholic Union Societies Political Club, made of many prominent Hamtramckans, to write a letter to the Common Council and *Newsweek*.

In part, the letter noted, "It is indeed fortunate for our community that the aforesaid article appeared before the tragic death of Bernice Onisko Otherwise Hamtramck, in addition to various inequities charged to its name, would have been probably listed with other localities where the lives of women are never safe during the late hours of night."

In late April, police thought they got a major break when a twenty-one-year-old Detroit man confessed to the murder. But the excitement was short-lived. A day after announcing the break, police rejected the confession as the "fabrication of an unbalanced mind," according to newspapers. No evidence was found to link the man to the murder, and, in fact, it was shown that he was in the town of Halfway, Michigan, when the crime was committed. Police exhausted every lead, but nothing materialized.

Time passed—weeks, months, finally a year. In March 1938, a one-year memorial mass was held at St. Ladislaus Church. Bernice's mother was there, and "she has not changed since the tragic incident," the *New Deal* newspaper reported. "The mere mention of the girl's name causes her to break down." The paper reported that she prays fervently that her daughter's killed would be caught.

He never was.

Deep in the files of the Hamtramck Police Department is the case report of the murder of Bernice Onisko. It is huge and contains a massive amount of information on the investigation. It also includes photos of the murder site that have not and never should be made public. Technically, the case is still an active investigation, although whoever the murderer was is almost certainly long dead. We can surmise that Onisko was the victim of a random encounter. That is the hardest type of murder to solve, since there is no connection between the victim and the perpetrator other than the crime. Further, this was long before the era of DNA testing, so the murderer slipped into the darkness of that Saturday night without leaving a trace that could be followed.

Bernice's mother likely never found peace in the wake of the tragedy, but she could take a modest degree of consolation that Bernice died in possession of her prayer book and rosary. As the *New Deal* reported in its last words on the case, "She met her maker with a soul cleansed."

Case No. 1937-2

Infanticide/Reduced to Manslaughter

In the eyes of the law, there's no question that Leona Maciejowicz was a killer and perhaps the worst sort of killer—a child murderer. But in a startling turnabout of events, in her case, mercy triumphed over the law.

The 1930s were not a particularly charitable time. The Great Depression was brutal for the working class, and morals were rigid, especially for young women. Maciejowicz, twenty-one, made the mistake of getting pregnant and not being married. Further, she refused to identify the father. That was not a crime, although at that time, it carried the stigma of one. It wasn't unusual for young ladies to suddenly disappear for months at a time under the pretense that they were "visiting relatives" as they completed their pregnancies in solitude and avoided bringing shame to the family.

But Maciejowicz had no real family. She was alone, and she delivered her baby herself in the bathtub. What happened next isn't exactly clear, except that she marched over to the police station with the baby, which she said had been born dead. But an inspection showed that there was a stab wound in the baby's head, extending from the rear up into the skull. She said she knew nothing of that and insisted the baby was stillborn. Maciejowicz was immediately taken to St. Francis Hospital, where she spent nearly a week recovering from the birth. Then she was transferred to the Women's Division of the Wayne County Jail. She was charged with first-degree murder by prosecutor Duncan McRea. Still, she maintained her innocence and would not identify the father. As she headed for trial in November 1937, she acquired the services of attorney Arthur Willard, who took her defense straight to the general public.

"No jury in the country could convict the girl of first degree murder in this case," he said. "The girl is not a murderer. Her record at Bohn Aluminum Company where she worked was spotless." He said Maciejowicz was "a victim of circumstances." Hard luck has dogged her since early childhood. Her mother died when she was in her early teens, and she got very little help from her father. For five years, she has been in the employ of a Hamtramck officer doing housework. When she became conscious of her pregnancy, she quit her job there and went to work in a factory to make more money and be somewhat prepared when the child came. She had no person to go to for support in her distressing condition.

"On the day of delivery she had awful pains. She was afraid to go to her landlady so she undertook to bear her baby by herself. She was in terrible agony, and I can't see how anyone can conceive that a girl in her mental condition could have premeditated the murder of her child.

"The daze in which she found herself at the time put a fear into her that probably was the force behind her wrapping the baby in a newspaper and hiding it in a dresser. After hiding the child, she went to the groceries for herself and upon her return found that the landlady had discovered the body. Traces of uremic poisoning have also been said to be found on the girl at the time she surrendered to authorities, which if true, would have a definite effect on her mental condition."

Quite a sales pitch, but apparently it was working. Willard said that residents of Hamtramck had offered to put up a $10,000 bond for Maciejowicz. She went to trial in March and, unsurprisingly, was found guilty of second-degree murder, which could have sent her to prison for years. But Wayne County circuit judge Allan Campbell sentenced her to probation. He was able to do that because attorney Willard asked for a new trial after Maciejowicz had been convicted. The judge agreed, and Maciejowicz pleaded guilty to manslaughter. It was under that charge that she was sentenced to probation.

Said Judge Campbell, "I have never in my life seen a girl who has gone through such hardships. Let us hope that she will get a new start in life. I hope that everyone will get together in aiding her. She deserves a chance."

Maciejowicz's case had attracted considerable attention even beyond Hamtramck. Locally, she received the support of other Hamtramck women who sympathized with her plight. She was viewed as a victim of her circumstances, pushed to commit a heinous act by an unforgiving society that condemned her for getting pregnant. Keep in mind that this was a time when municipal corruption was tolerated, and the crimes committed during Prohibition just a few years earlier were openly accepted. Yet "moral" failings, like illegitimate pregnancy or even divorce, usually drew harsh rebukes from the general public.

Even the *Detroit Medical News* noted her plight. It wrote in an editorial on November 1, 1937, "That this girl, in this circumstance, mentally overwhelmed, does such a thing is understandable. She is not on trial. It is society that should do groveling penance.

"Sheklov, or Sherwood Anderson, or Somerset Maugham could truly delineate what went on in the girl's mind. When her baby kicked inside of her and awakened her in the night, we wonder if she prayed. What a living hell she went through for nine months. No one to advise. Obviously no family, no doctor, no religious affiliation to whom she might unburden; no one, nothing to aid, to relieve."

It went on with great emotion to attempt to express the hopeless situation that pushed the young mother to commit the ultimate crime. She was a woman "with less help than given a dog…alone in a room in a rooming house."

On her release from jail on probation, the *New Deal* newspaper noted that she had changed her name and, with boldness or lack of forethought, revealed the new name but did note that "sympathetic local citizens are giving her the rest and peace of mind she so richly deserves after the harrowing months she spent in expectancy and in the Wayne County Jail."

And so ended the public life of Leona Maciejowicz. She quickly fell off the pages of the newspapers and out of view of the community. How she spent the rest of her life has not been recorded.

CASE NO. 1937-2

Homicide

The murder of Leo Gutowski, also known as Leo Gutt, looked like another mob hit. His battered body was found in an orchard at Lone Pine Road and Orchard Lake Road in West Bloomfield Township, which at that time was a remote rural area about twenty miles northwest of Hamtramck. Police theorized that he "had been taken for a ride" by gang members. But that theory quickly fell apart.

Gutowski was thirty years old in October 1937, when he died. He lived in a rooming house at 2720 Trowbridge Street and was employed at the Dodge Main factory. And he had the reputation of being a ladies' man, which had been a source of contention. In fact, fellow residents of the rooming house where Gutowski lived said he had been involved in a vicious fight with another man, Stanley Karwowski of Evaline Street, on the night he disappeared.

Gutowski's body was found the next morning by a farmhand who was cutting corn stalks. The farmhand notified the Oakland County's Sheriff's Office. Gutowski was identified by a pawn ticket, keys, an Old Timers Club button and several laundry tickets found in his pockets.

From the state of Gutowski's body, it was clear that he had been severely beaten before he was shot once in the back of the head. His blood-soaked hat was found nearby in the bushes. Also, there were footprints in the ground around the body. While these did not prove to be a clue in identifying the killer, they did disprove that it was Karwowski. Karwowski and Gutowski did have a fierce battle in the rooming house, which resulted in Karwowski getting a couple of teeth knocked out and Gutowski suffering a knife wound to his arm. But Karwowski had the lower portion of a leg amputated earlier, and the tracks found near Gutowski's body indicated that whoever made them had a normal walking stride. That did not preclude the possibility that Gutowski's killer had been a hired gun. Karwowski and Gutowski battled over the perception that Gutowski had made a pass at Karwowski's girlfriend, and police pursued the jealous lover theory. But that also led nowhere. Further, there was no indication that Gutowski had any criminal contacts. He had been a suspect in a robbery of a store the previous spring but was not charged with anything.

Despite the dead ends, police boldly predicted they would crack the case soon. "We'll have the murder of Leo Gutowski within a week," police captain John Sikorski said. "We have discarded the theory that Gutowski came to his death at the hands of a jealous man. We switched our investigation to another channel and we're satisfied that we have the right track this time."

Maybe not.

Weeks and then months went by, and there were no arrests, and the killer of Leo Gutowski was never caught.

Case No. 1937-3

Homicide

Bars and brawls are a natural combination, but when a multi-bar crosstown drinking spree turns into vicious killing, it attracts front-page attention in the newspapers.

Such was the story of Paul Snyder, twenty-six, of Watson Avenue in Detroit. He and his friends Jim Simpson and Sam Insalaco set off on a drinking spree on the evening of Saturday, June 19, 1937. They started drinking in Detroit and made their way to the Klinger Inn on Klinger and Leuschner Streets on the far south side of town. At about 2:00 a.m., the three men left the bar and staggered down Conant Avenue. As they passed a parked car, one of two occupants in the car began taunting the trio. They responded, and one of the men in the car got out and started fighting with Snyder. In the course of the fight, the attacker pulled a knife and slashed Snyder six times, including inflicting a fatal wound to the neck. His two friends stood by too drunk to come to his defense. They couldn't even describe the attacker to police.

This would have proved to be a major detriment to the police investigation, but the police got a tip that the killer was John L. King of Helen Avenue in Detroit. The identity of the man who was with King was not known, but he did not participate in the fatal fight and was not wanted by police. At least that is what they said. Ordinarily he would be sought as a witness, which leads to the question, was he actually the tipster?

In any case, King was already known to Detroit police. He had been sentenced to a five- to twenty-five-year term in Jackson prison on an armed robbery charge. Police knew where he lived and staked out his house. It was several days before he showed up, but when he did, he was arrested. He was arraigned on murder charges that were later reduced to manslaughter by the Wayne County assistant prosecutor.

CASE NO. 1937-4

Homicide

It was described in the press at the time as "one of the most gory deaths in the annals of Hamtramck crime." Indeed, the story that spilled out of the mouth of young Mitchell Karaskiewicz looked like something from a sleazy, gory horror movie.

Karaskiewicz was only twenty in January 1937, when he faced an unrelenting barrage of police questions. It wasn't a new experience for him. He had already done eighteen months of a one- to five-year sentence for car theft. After being paroled from the Detroit House of Corrections, he was picked up by police numerous times on suspicion of a variety of petty crimes but never faced charges—until this one.

The scene of this crime was the old Kanas Hall on Conant Street, just a few blocks from Karaskiewicz's home on Moran Street near Commor Street. At that time, there were several halls scattered across Hamtramck. They usually consisted of a bar, drinking area, a kitchen and ballroom where dancing could be held. In some halls, there was a large theater area with a stage upstairs. Parties, political rallies, dances and musical presentations were often held. Kanas Hall was typical, a fairly large redbrick building. On Saturday, January 23, 1937, a dance was being held there. Karaskiewicz had already been to a party held in Warren, a city just north of Hamtramck, and didn't arrive at Kanas Hall until 1:30 a.m. on Sunday. He told police that he went to the hall because his sister and some friends were going to be there.

Karaskiewicz was acquainted with his victim, Paul Kolak, who was a watchman at the hall. When the dance finally broke up early Sunday

Kanas Hall on Conant Avenue was the site of one of Hamtramck's most notorious murders. In 1997, it was turned into rubble when directly struck by a tornado.

morning, dance organizers asked Kolak if they should take Karaskiewicz with them, as everyone else had left.

"Oh, no, he's a friend of mine," Kolak said.

It took police four days to pry the story of what happened next out of Karaskiewicz. The following is his statement:

> *I talked with Kolak at the bar in the basement. I then went to his room [in the hall] and fell asleep. Later, Kolak woke me and asked what I was doing. I told him I was the one who helped him at the hall. He told me I better get out, and he spilled a glass of beer on me. I grabbed for the glass in his hand and started to run upstairs. He chased me and finally caught me beside the stage. We fought a while, and I must have pushed him because he fell to the bottom of the stairs and hit his head. I was scared and ran to the check room next to the ticket office and hid there for ten or fifteen minutes.*
>
> *I finally came out and found him lying in blood. I saw him get up and pick up a coat. He used it to wipe his face of the blood. I asked him, "Are you hurt?" and he came up after me. I ran to the other side of the stage. He got ahold of me there, but I jerked away and ran to the front. He came after*

*me and caught me. I tore away and pushed him into a pipe, and he fell.
Then as I tried to run back into the hall, he grabbed for my legs, got ahold
of one and held on so tight one of my shoes came off. I took my shoe away
and left through the side door.*

*It must have been late because people were going to church. I went to
a candy store at 11521 Conant Avenue and bought two bottles of pop. I
drank them and went home.*

Kolak's body was found at 10:00 a.m. on Sunday by Stanley Baczinski, who was also a watchman who helped Kolak. Baczinski called hall owner Joseph Maj, who called police.

Apparently, police found a phenomenal amount of blood and something else—Karaskiewicz's coat and a receipt with his address on it. Police made a quick trip to Karaskiewicz's home, where they found him in bed, his hand covered with blood.

CASE NO. 1938-1

Homicide

Joseph Mushro drank too much.

"We were so drunk we didn't know we had shot and killed a man until we read the newspapers the next day," Mushro told police after he and partners in crime Thomas McCarthy and Joseph Staniszewski were arrested for the murder of poolroom attendant Alex Romansyshin, fifty. Romansyshin was in the Original Billiards Hall at 8630 Jos. Campau Avenue, near the Dodge Main factory, when it was robbed at 5:45 a.m. on Saturday, March 12, 1938. Mushro and his pals were brandishing guns when they entered the pool hall and began ordering people around. They shot at those who didn't move fast enough. Romansyshin, who was believed to have been partially deaf, didn't move fast enough. He was shot. One of the gunmen also fired several bullets into the ceiling, awakening Michael Penarowski, who lived in a room above the pool hall. He ran downstairs and right into the robbers, who knocked him cold with a pistol butt. Michael Godyk, a patron at the pool hall, was also knocked out with a pistol. Everyone else in the place was forced to put their money on a pool table. Accounts vary about how much that was, but it was in the area of a couple hundred dollars.

With all the commotion, someone called police, and patrolmen Robert Bargowski and John Abrams pulled up in a patrol wagon as the thieves were fleeing from the front and rear doors. Abrams chased two of the men for six blocks, firing at them repeatedly but missing. The men escaped, but an intensive statewide manhunt was launched, leading to their arrests.

They were tried for murder in Wayne County Circuit Court the following August. Mushro was identified by police as the triggerman, but he said he didn't know anything about it.

"I had twelve bottles of beer and a quart of whiskey with the boys," he said. "I remember we decided to hold up the place for some easy dough. We all had guns. But I can't remember shooting."

All three men were convicted of murder and sentenced to life in prison, a fact that seemed to be lost on Mushro. "I'm going to serve my time and get out of there as soon as possible," he said. "I'll behave. Maybe it'll only be 12 years. Maybe I'll learn a trade in prison and then I'll go straight when I get out."

Maybe.

CASE NO. 1938-2

Homicide/Robbery/Remorse

For John W. Deering, enough was finally enough. After a life of crime culminating in the murder of businessman Oliver Meredith, he was ready to call it quits for good. No, he wasn't going to swear off crime and go straight. He wanted to set an appointment with a firing squad.

"I prefer to be shot," he said when offered the choice between hanging or a firing squad.

Deering's life of crime began when he was seventeen, and he served eight years in San Quentin. Three weeks after he got out, he committed a robbery that netted him twelve more years in Folsom Prison. But that wasn't enough for Deering. After being released from Folsom, he committed a robbery in Portland, Oregon, and shot a policeman while getting away. In the process, he was shot but managed to take refuge in a swamp, where he cauterized his wounds with a burning rag.

Not long afterward, he fatally stabbed a homeless person who he said had tried to molest him in a boxcar somewhere out "west." Prior to arriving in Hamtramck, Deering robbed and killed Salt Lake City businessman Oliver R. Meredith. Deering made his way to Hamtramck, where he and some gang members robbed the City Finance Co., where they escaped with all of $100.

But he had done better on his own. When police arrested him at a bar at Jos. Campau and Belmont Street on July 28, 1938, he told them he had committed ten robberies locally, escaping with $7,700. And, by the way, he had murdered Meredith in Utah.

Apparently, the booze had cleared Deering's head, and he had come to understand that he was a hopeless criminal who would never change. He just wanted to die. He said he would not fight extradition to Utah and would plead guilty there to avoid a possibly long trial. He just wanted "to get it over with," he said. Understandably, the police were skeptical. They thought that Deering wanted to get back to Utah, where he might renege on his promised plea and try to put up a stronger defense, even though he faced a death sentence there. But they were wrong. When Deering was told that he was going to get a trial after all, he threw fit. He yelled that he was being "double-crossed" and wanted to be done with everything.

But he got the trial, and a guilty verdict was delivered by the jury. As we leave Deering, he was on death row awaiting his final peace.

CASE NO. 1937–38-3

Homicide/Bank Robbery

Michigan became a state in 1837. Nine years later, the residents found their collective conscience and banned capital punishment. So, how is it that the last execution carried out in Michigan occurred in 1938?

Ask the government. Had it been up to Michigan governor Frank Murphy, there never would have been an execution in Michigan, but federal law supersedes state law, and the state was ordered to hang Anthony "Tony" Chebatoris. Records do not indicate that Chebatoris was from Hamtramck, but he had an association with the city through his partner in crime, Jack Gracy. Gracy lived at 3874 Comstock Street with his mother and stepfather. Gracy was well known to Hamtramck police for a long string of crimes that landed him in prison in Jackson, Michigan. It was there that he met Chebatoris and formed an alliance that ultimately led to an ill-conceived and poorly executed attempt to rob the Chemical Savings Bank in Midland, Michigan, about 125 miles northwest of Hamtramck. In the late summer of 1937, Gracy cased the bank and thought it was an easy mark. The day of the robbery, the two men drove from Hamtramck in separate cars to Corunna, Michigan, about 45 miles from Midland. Gracy was driving a stolen car, and Chebatoris was driving a car owned by a man both robbers knew. They ditched the stolen car in Corunna and drove together to Midland.

At about 11:30 a.m. on Wednesday, September 29, 1937, they entered the bank. Manager Clarence Macomber was by the front having a conversation with his twenty-two-year-old daughter, Clair, who also worked for the bank. Gracy moved first, pulling a .38-caliber gun and pushing it into Macomber's ribs. But Macomber grabbed the gun, and the two began to struggle. Chebatoris shot Macomber, and cashier Paul Bywater rushed in to aid Macomber and was shot by Chebatoris. Their plans having gone horribly wrong, Chebatoris and Gracy ran out of the bank to their getaway car. Gracy jumped into the passenger seat as Chebatoris stepped on the gas. At the same time, Frank Hardy, a dentist, was in his office above a store next to the bank. He heard the shots and realized it was being robbed. Remember this was the era of Bonnie and Clyde and John Dillinger, whose hobby was robbing banks. So, Hardy was not shocked that someone would try to rob the bank downstairs. He grabbed a .38-caliber rifle he kept in the office and pushed its barrel though the window screen and spotted the speeding getaway car. He fired several times. The first shot hit the car's fender, the second hit the car's door and the third ripped through the car's rear window, striking Chebatoris in the arm. He lost control of the car, which swerved across the street, crashing into a parked car. The impact sent Gracy flying out of the car and onto the street. Chebatoris got out of the car and went to Gracy, helping him up.

Together they looked for the source of the shots, but all they saw was a man wearing a uniform standing on a nearby corner. It was truck driver Henry Porter, but Chebatoris might have mistaken him for a police officer. In any case, Chebatoris shot, wounding him. Desperate, Chebatoris and Gracy attempted to carjack a woman driving by with a baby in the car. She sped away, and Chebatoris fired at her car but apparently did not do any damage. Rapidly running out of options, the pair ran to a bridge over the Tittabawassee River. They tried to commandeer a passing truck, but as Gracy stood on the truck's running board, he was hit in the head by another shot fired by Hardy. Reports said the back of his head was blown away.

Chebatoris fled on foot, running along the Pere Marquette Railroad tracks. He attempted to hijack two more vehicles before he was caught by a group of men who held him until the county sheriff arrived and arrested him. Chebatoris was charged with murder and convicted after a three-day trial in which the prosecution called thirty-four witnesses and the defense called none. He was found guilty and sentenced to death. His execution was set for July 8, 1938. But Michigan did not have a death penalty. However, Chebatoris was convicted under the new Federal Bank Robbery Act, which provided for the death penalty. And technically, although Michigan had banned the death penalty in 1846, it left in place a provision to implement execution in cases of treason. That was later repealed and still later reimposed. Bottom line: Chebatoris marched up the gallows stairs and came down through the trap door.

One newspaper referred to him as "an arrogant Pole from Hamtramck," but it isn't clear if he actually lived in the city. There was a close enough connection to warrant a story on the front page of Hamtramck's *New Deal* newspaper announcing his execution.

Incidentally, his cause of death is technically considered a homicide.

5

THE NOT-SO-FABULOUS '40s

T he 1940s dawned in peace.
"All Quite," proclaimed the headline on the *Citizen* newspaper on January 5, 1940. "It Was a Dull New Year for Police, but They Didn't Mind It," the subhead stated.

"So far as Hamtramck police were concerned the night between the departure of 1939 and the arrival of 1940 was just another work shift, not marred by any actual work," the story related.

Not a single arrest was made on the last day of 1939 or the first day of 1940. That, for Hamtramck, was newsworthy. But it wouldn't last. In fact, the world was already in the midst of great change. World War II had started in September 1939, which had an enormous impact on Hamtramck. At that time, Hamtramck's population stood at about 49,830 people, and about 80 percent of them were from Poland or of Polish descent. Many had close relatives living in Poland, directly in the gunsights of Hitler's invading troops. While the rest of the United States was technically neutral regarding the war in Europe, there was no question among the people of Hamtramck that they were under attack.

The bond between Hamtramck and Poland was reinforced in early February 1940, when General Joseph Haller visited the city. Haller was a Polish military hero who served as an ambassador of sorts, traveling around the world drumming up support for Poland. His visit to Hamtramck drew thousands who came to greet him and follow him as he toured sites around the city, including the Dodge factory, St. Florian Church and, appropriately, a couple Polish veteran halls. Inevitably, America's attention was turning to thoughts of war, which would only increase as time went by.

But that didn't mean that Hamtramckans had suddenly found the light and realized the wickedness of their ways. The old ways die hard, and the corruption that had been ingrained in Hamtramck society had deep roots. Not even the threat of Adolf Hitler could unite all Hamtramckans in the cause of goodness. In March 1940, forty-six persons were arrested in raids on five "houses of ill repute." All faced charges of "loitering in an establishment selling liquor without a license or loitering in a house of ill repute." Impressive, but there was a stale note to the whole affair as if this were a sad song that we had heard before. Indeed, one of the raids was personally conducted by police commissioner Raymond Matyniak and police chief Barney Nowicki. And all the raids were planned after Wayne County prosecutor Duncan McCrea, who had been charged with accepting protection money, said that Hamtramck police were involved in the racket.

"I want a thorough investigation begun in regard to this matter," Mayor Walter Kanar wrote in a letter to Matyniak. "I shall expect prompt action in this matter, as the public is entitled to all protection."

Hence the raids.

More would follow just as many had preceded it. And all had virtually the same result, which was essentially nothing. They made great headlines and talking points for politicians but didn't put a dent in the rampant corruption that had become the hallmark of Hamtramck. Not coincidentally, Matyniak announced in 1942 that he was running for mayor. His primary opposition was a new political figure—Dr. Stephen Skrzycki, a popular local doctor. Both took reformist stances, although Matyniak focused more on finances and city operations, while Skrzycki had a more moralistic perspective.

"Before I agreed to become a candidate I insisted on and secured a pledge from the organizations who offered me their support that there would be no cellar and beer parties and the like," Skrzycki said. "Upon that condition I became a candidate."

Almost simultaneously, acting mayor Anthony Tenerowicz indicated that he was considering summarily firing several police officers who had admitted to accepting bribes to protect vice rackets in the city. It didn't provoke a major reaction, but it was a reminder that the tide of corruption had not receded yet. But something was changing, even if it was hard to identify clearly. It was as if the fire that sparked Hamtramck's lively social, political and even criminal scene was fading. The primary election that pitted Skrzycki against Matyniak was labeled "one of the quietest, oddest

Mayoral candidate Dr. Stephen Skrzycki surrounded by supporters as he files his petitions to run for office of mayor. That's long-time city clerk Walter Gajewski ready to take the documents. Dr. Skrzycki ushered in an era of clean government.

and most unpredictable elections in recent Hamtramck history" by the *Citizen* newspaper. "By far the most outstanding feature was the serenity of the occasion. No campaign literature, no signs near booths, no political workers—noting marred the day."

The situation was so unusual that the *Citizen* newspaper was moved to run a rare front-page editorial. "No one rang doorbells to get people to vote, no one who did vote had to run the gauntlet of signs or zealous workers shouting the praise of their favorites, or try through a drunken brawl at a booth—or face a critical stare of a challenger inside a booth....It all happened because two candidates for the office of mayor decided, upon the urging of the people, to conduct a nice, clean campaign."

Skrzycki went on to win the general election by a hefty margin of 7,616 votes to Matyniak's 4,446.

But the *Citizen* might have been more perceptive than even its veteran editorial staff realized at the time. The words "upon the urging of the

Police commissioner Raymond Matyniak watches his wife fill out a document as he prepares to run for mayor of Hamtramck against Dr. Stephen Skrzycki. Election worker Hattie Blaszczak (*left*) looks on.

people" were tremendously revealing, for the people had enough. They were tired of the continuous corruption, crime and seemingly never-ending police raids that were more for show than substance. Perhaps it was because there were bigger things to worry about. World War II was just gearing up for the United States as a whole, and the threat to the entire nation was becoming more evident. Perhaps, but it was becoming evident that Hamtramckans were fed up with scandals. They wanted peace not just for their nation but also for their neighborhood. Skrzycki embodied that. While he bore an uncanny resemblance to Adolf Hitler, he demonstrated no fascist tendencies, although one of his first actions in office was to attempt to fire some forty or so city employees to deal with still another of the city's financial crises that occurred regularly. He later backed down.

Skrzycki's administration lasted ten years and was noted for nothing in particular. And that was good. Once Skrzycki was established in office, reports of police raids on blind pigs, illegal liquor operations and houses of prostitution began to fade simply because those entities were losing popularity. That's not to say there were no bumps along the road. In July 1946, the Hamtramck Public School board was embroiled in scandal when four members were accused of taking bribes to appoint people to jobs or approve the hiring of job applicants. Further, some teachers in the system charged that the only way they could get a promotion was to bribe school board members. The scope of the investigation expanded into questionable use of funds for certain programs for children by the school board, which led the state to appoint an administrator of the public school system. As that was happening, a new civic group was being formed that was dedicated to cleaning corruption in the city. It was made up of teachers, homeowners, businesspeople and anyone who paid taxes in Hamtramck. What, if anything, they actually accomplished isn't clear, but it was a symbol of how the people wanted to do something, anything, about the corruption.

School board member Pauline Zuk became a key figure in the school scandal but not as a suspect. In fact, she took part in a scheme to prove the corruption was real by accepting a bribe from someone who wanted a school job and promptly turning the money over to Hamtramck judge Nicholas Gronkowski. "I risked my reputation because when I got on the board and found out what was going on. I had to make a choice," she said. "I had to decide to be part of tough situation or to fight it....If we don't succeed in cleaning this up we are going to be back where we were 20 years ago."

She did succeed, and Hamtramck moved forward into a new era. Indictments were handed down, and the school system was reformed. The late 1940s and early 1950s were catatonic compared to the previous two decades. From time to time, right through the 1970s, there were raids on illegal gambling operations and houses of prostitution but even that became rarer. The murder rate dipped compared to earlier years and continued into the 1960s, when all of America was wracked by social pains as the civil rights movement shook the nation. And as long as there are people, even calm, usually reasonable people, they will occasionally kill each other.

Case No. 1942-1; 1980-1

Homicide

In the history of Hamtramck crime and criminals, no one can compare with Roman Usiondek.

He truly was in a class by himself—the lowest class imaginable. Usiondek appeared on the police radar screen long before radar was invented. He was born around 1917, and before he was even eighteen years old, he was involved in the growing number of gangs in Hamtramck. His street name was "Crutchie," although why has not been recorded. He was also known as Ray Shondek and Robert Burns and Joe Blake. He was sentenced to the Boys' Industrial School for breaking and entering. Out of jail, he led a juvenile gang and was known for his violence and bravado. "He would fight with sticks, clubs, rocks and feet," an old-time colleague in crime remembered. He was fearless and treated a gun as just another tool to use. He was arrested several times for being a disorderly person, and in 1936, he graduated to a higher level of crime when he was convicted of armed robbery and sentenced to twenty years in Jackson prison. He was pardoned four years later but was back in the slammer after only six months on a parole violation. But he got out after six months.

In 1942, he turned to murder for the first time, apparently. He was indicted for killing a small-time gangster named Frank Reid but was not convicted. That set the stage for what was to come—one of the most notorious murders in the history of Hamtramck.

Peter Kubert and his wife, Sophie, owned and operated a bar on Carpenter Avenue in May 1942. In many ways, the Kuberts were the ideal bar owners. They didn't just serve drinks in their popular bar at 3216 Carpenter Street, right on Hamtramck's border with north Detroit. They were everybody's pal. They were well known around town for a variety of community activities. It seemed like all of Hamtramck liked the Kuberts.

It all came to an end at about 1:30 a.m. on Saturday, May 23, 1942, when Usionek and his crew of cutthroats culminated a night of crime by invading the Kuberts' bar. They had been hitting bars in the area for some time—Columbia Café on Jacob Street, Bill's Bar on Conant Avenue and another bar on Lumpkin Street, along with about fifteen others.

Earlier that evening, at about 9:45 p.m., they robbed Emil Miles of $110 at his bar on St. Aubin Street at the other end of Hamtramck. Police did get a radio call on the robbery and gave chase to the Usiondek gang's

Peter Kubert (*right*) receives an honorary key to the city from Judge John D. Krause while visiting Manistee, Michigan. Not only was Kubert a popular bar owner, but he was also a well-respected citizen for his many community involvements. That made his murder even more painful for the community.

car but lost it in heavy traffic. At 12:30 a.m., the robbers hit Sonny's Café at 12424 Van Dyke Road in nearby Detroit. There the take was richer, as they escaped with $1,600. Whether the crew was drunk with success or liquor is questionable, but the thieves decided to go for a third hit that night. And the folks who were in Kubert's bar when the robbers walked through the door about an hour after leaving Sonny's Café said they could smell liquor on their breaths through the handkerchiefs each was wearing to hide their faces. About seventeen people were in the bar just as Kubert was getting ready to close. The robbers wasted no time, pulling guns and forcing the patrons into a back room. They cleared out the cash register but found it contained only about $600. For some reason, the robbers believed Kubert had $3,000 on the premises, and Usiondek demanded more. Kubert, apparently unimpressed with gunmen, pointed to some small change on the bar. In response, one of the gunmen fired at Kubert, hitting him in the right arm and abdomen. Though wounded, Kubert dived for his own gun behind the bar and got six shots off at the robbers, but only one found a mark, hitting Henry Hill but not injuring him seriously. He later became a state witness. Kubert survived the attack. Sophie said he never even lost consciousness and spoke of the attack repeatedly, saying the robber had threatened to "shoot his guts out" if he failed to produce more money.

He was taken to St. Francis Hospital just a few blocks away. At first, he seemed to recover, but peritonitis set in, and he died at 12:12 a.m. the following Friday.

Funeral services were held at Transfiguration Church in north Detroit and were conducted by Father Simon Kilar, a personal friend. News of Kubert's brutal shooting and death sparked outrage in the community. The Hamtramck Common Council took the extraordinary step of offering $500 for providing information leading to the capture of Kubert's killers.

"As long as these killers roam the streets, no one in Hamtramck is safe," said council president Walter J. Serement. "If that amount isn't enough, I'm sure the businessmen of this community will spontaneously join in making the reward larger by contributing to the fund. Mr. Kubert was a fine citizen, an asset to this city, and certainly not deserving of the fate which was meted out by merciless bandits."

Three teams of detectives—two from Hamtramck and one from Detroit—were immediately put on the case and began to produce results quickly. A witness was found who said he saw two of the robbers leaving the bar, and one removed the handkerchief from his face, exposing a prominent mole. That led them to Rudolph Maday, thirty-five, of Milwaukee Street just south of Hamtramck. The other suspect was identified as Emil Jaworski, twenty-six, of Danforth Street in Hamtramck. Maday had a connection to Usiondek. Both had been suspects in the killing of Frank Reid, a small-time Detroit gangster. According to witnesses of that shooting, Usiondek walked up to Reid, who was standing near a café on Woodward Avenue, asked for a cigarette and match and then pulled a gun and shot him in the face.

Pete Kubert promoted his place as "Hamtramck's Finest" in a newspaper ad.

That in turn led police to Stephen Janowski, thirty-seven, of Carrie Street and James Lynch (Lesinski), thirty-four, of Moenart Street, both in Detroit. All had extensive police records. Maday was first arrested in March 1922 and had been arrested every year thereafter on one charge or another. Lynch was first arrested in 1923 and, in 1936, drew a ten- to twenty-year sentence in Jackson prison for armed robbery. Jaworski also had his share of trouble with the law but, as it turned out, not with the Kubert case. All of the men were intensely questioned by police to such an extent that Jaworski filed a $50,000 lawsuit again the police for their rough treatment. But there was no question that these were tough guys. Ordinarily, suspects are arraigned in the community where the crime occurred. But these men were arraigned in Detroit. It was felt that transporting them from jail in Detroit to the Hamtramck court posed too great of a risk, as they would likely try to escape.

In January 1943, Usiondek, Lynch, Jaworski and Madaj went on trial before Wayne County Circuit Court judge Theodore J. Richter for the robbery and murder of Kubert. Henry Hill, part of the gang, was not charged with Kubert's death and served as a key witness for the prosecution. He was later tried for an unrelated armed robbery. A jury of eight women and five men heard the case and had little difficulty reaching a verdict. Usiondek, Maday and Lynch were found guilty and given life sentences.

Jaworski was acquitted, as he was able to prove that he was elsewhere when the Kubert robbery and killing took place.

The *Detroit Free Press* newspaper noted that Judge Richter set a record in sentencing the trio just one minute after the verdict was returned. They each got terms of life in prison in solitary confinement and at hard labor.

However, even before being found guilty and sentenced to prison, Usiondek already made it known that he was not interested in spending his life in prison. In December 1942, while incarcerated in Wayne County Jail, he and seven other inmates were thrown into the jail "dungeon" for engineering an escape attempt. Somehow, the group had got ahold of a saw or saws and cut through a set of bars on the inner cell jail window and in the jail shower. How they got the saws into the jail and what happened to them remains a mystery. Also, a fifty-foot rope made from bedding was found in the prisoners' ward. However, Undersheriff William D. Ryan said the prisoners had not come close to escaping, for there was an even sturdier set of bars on the outside windows. That would have blocked their way. So, Usiondek and his pals went to trial and were duly convicted and sent to prison.

But this woeful tale is far from over.

Sophie Kubert continued to run the bar for several more years before it finally closed. The building had several more owners through the years, until it was demolished in 2018. And the memory of Peter Kubert faded, although it was thrust into the headlines again nearly forty years after his death. But there is a long, torturous road leading to that point in history. The first stop along the way is December 1950, when police finally caught up with Steve Marek. We haven't mentioned him before, but he was part of the gang that burst into Kubert's bar that night in 1942. Marek had eluded police, at least for eight years, when Hamtramck police Captain George Knuckles got a tip that Marek was at a house on Danforth Street in Hamtramck. Knuckles sent fifteen officers to surround the house and force Marek out. They did, but he put up a battle. At this time, Usiondek was still in prison but not for too much longer. And if anything, he had grown even meaner behind bars.

In December 1953, he was back on the front pages of the newspapers with a new exploit. This time, he was one of thirteen prisoners who stole an acetylene torch that was being used by employees of the Chicago Bridge & Iron Co. on a water tower and cut through three metal screens in a storm sewer to crawl about 250 yards and escape from Jackson prison. They were the first prisoners to tunnel out of Jackson, the world's largest walled prison. Once free of the prison, the group broke into the house of a former guard two miles from the prison. They tied up homeowner Glenn Milliman and

Long after Pete Kubert's bar closed, it found new life as Shananigan's Bar and served drinks into the twenty-first century. The building has since been demolished.

his wife and stole an automatic pistol. They then packed themselves into a car and drove off to the city of Jackson. There, seven of the escapees got out at the New York Central railroad station. The other six drove off toward Napoleon, a small town about nine miles southeast of Jackson. But they didn't get far. Milliman had broken free and went to a neighbor's house and called the state police. They were on the trail of the escapees and chased them on Highway M50 before they overturned the car. The prisoners' date with freedom lasted all of three hours.

Meanwhile, an intense manhunt began for the remaining escapees. They were a motley group made of murderers, kidnappers and robbers. But Usiondek was likely the worst. Detroit senior inspector Walter S. Wyrod, who led the manhunt that was organized immediately after the escape, said Usiondek was "a psychopathic killer." That claim was supported by three of the escapees, Virgil Lane, a robber; Edward Emrick, a robber/killer; and Daniel Bousha, a kidnapper, who all said they were afraid of Usiondek—and so were the lawmen. At the trial for killing Pete Kubert, Usiondek vowed to get revenge against all who were responsible for his conviction. That included A. Tom Pasieczny, who was assistant prosecutor at the trial. "I'll be back and you'll be number one on my list," Usiondek told Pasieczny when he was sentenced to life in prison. On hearing Usiondek was on the loose, Pasieczny told police he was leaving Detroit "indefinitely" and did not say where he was going. Police provided protection to Sophie Kubert and others who had been witnesses at the Kubert murder trial. A warning was also given to the public to keep their house doors locked and not open them to strangers. Police also advised motorists to check the back seats of their cars before entering them and to lock cars when not using them.

Six teams of Hamtramck detectives were assigned to the case, and three scout cars were equipped with sawed-off shotguns for police to carry.

"Usiondek is a cold-blooded murderer who swore vengeance against all witness who testified against him at his trial," said Hamtramck police captain Walter Jaros. "Unless he had softened during his years in prison—and his escape proves he has not—I fear he will carry out his threat."

Usiondek and four other escapees broke into the house of Joseph Watts. Mrs. Watts was there with a friend, Helen Gilbert, and the escapees forced them to fix food and coffee for them. The men also took baths and shaved and stole all of Mr. Watts clothes. But notably, neither of the women were harmed. The gang was at the Wattses' house for about two hours, when Don Peck, a friend of Gilbert, arrived. He was going to be her date for a Christmas party. The gang forced Watts and Gilbert to be their drivers for their planned ride to Detroit. The women later told police that they were treated "with decency" by their kidnappers. After a drive of several hours crossing the area, Usiondek and fellow escapee Robert Dowling got out of the car at Seven Mile Road and Southfield Road. The three other escapees had the women drive them to Joy Road and Wyoming Street on Detroit's west side, where they got out and even gave the woman one dollar for gas. Watts and Gates drove to a nearby gas station, where they called the police.

The three men were caught a short time later at the house of Joseph Rocco, an ex-convict who had been a member of the Alcide (Frenchy) Benoit gang. Rocco claimed the three forced him to provide shelter. The police weren't so sure but what mattered most was that they captured the three escapes.

Two of the remaining escapees had stayed behind in Jackson. One was caught later that night near a hotel in the city. The next day, the other man crawled out of a coal bin and surrendered to police.

That left only Usiondek and Dowling on the loose. They stole a car in Detroit and drove to Richmond, Indiana, where they checked into the Mack Hotel in downtown Richmond. Alert police officers there spotted the car and learned that two men fitting the description of Usiondek and Dowling had checked in the previous night. Three officers confronted Dowling and Usiondek in their room. When Captain John Rizio asked Dowling for identification, he replied, "This is my identification" and reached for his hat on a dresser. It concealed a gun, but before Dowling could use it, Rizio was on top of him and disarmed him. The two other officers immediately jumped on Usiondek, who was sitting on a bed, and placed him in handcuffs.

That ended that chapter in the story of Roman Usiondek, but the story is still far from done.

Jump ahead to January 1965. Usiondek is still in prison, but he found a loophole that was bigger than the sewer he had crawled out of twelve years earlier. He asked for a new trial in the killing of Peter Kubert based on the fact that he had been found "guilty as charged" by the jury in 1943. However, Michigan law specifies that the jury determine the degree of murder someone can be convicted of. Usiondek was granted a new trial and immediately pleaded guilty to a charge of second-degree murder. Circuit court judge Carl Weideman sentenced Usiondek to fourteen to eighteen years in prison, but he was given credit for time served. So, he was out, but again, not for too long.

Two years later, on July 14, 1967, at 4:00 a.m., an alarm went off, and police were summoned to JoAnn's Supper Club at 6700 East Eight Mile Road in Detroit. It's a fairly modest place on the corner. Behind are rows of middle-class houses. The alarm automatically alerted police, and the alarm company called the club to verify the signal. At JoAnn's, night porter Fernando Jamie, fifty-three, answered and said all was well. But police officer George King and a representative from the alarm company pound on the door. Jamie answered from inside, assuring him that nothing was wrong. But King could see through the window and spots several people moving around. King smashed the window and yelled to Jamie to get out of the way. Jamie yelled back that he was being held hostage by three men who broke in. And then three shots were fired from inside.

King immediately radioed for backup, and nine scout cars sped to the scene. Minutes passed, and the side door was thrown open. A man—Edward Emrick—ran from the building, shooting. King responded, getting two rounds off. Emrick ran across Eight Mile Road to a parking lot and then collapsed, dead. At the back of JoAnn's, patrolman Stanley Stopczynski broke the glass window out of the door. He saw a second man—our boy Roman Usiondek—holding Jamie. Stopczynski fired four times, striking Usiondek once in the stomach. He fell to the floor. Soon, building owner Joseph Jarackas arrived on-site with the building keys. They entered and found Usiondek lying on the floor. At the same time, a third man ran out of the building. He was chased by police and brought down in an open space a short way away. He was unhurt and identified as George Patros, fifty-three, an ex-con with a record of robbery, kidnapping and burglary.

Jamie was unhurt and told police that the three men used a ruse to get him to open the door. They pounded on the door, screaming that there was a fire on the roof. Coincidentally, there had been a fire at the club a year earlier, so Jamie was frightened. He opened the door and was rushed by the three. They said it was a stickup and ordered him to lie on the floor. But when Jamie opened the door, he automatically set off the alarm, summoning police. Usiondek was taken to Detroit Receiving Hospital, where he identified himself as Ray Preston. A check of fingerprints soon exposed his true identity.

Emerick, sixty-five, who died at the scene, was an old cohort of Usoindek. They had been among the thirteen men who had escaped from Jackson prison in 1953. Emrick, a Hamtramckan, was a lifelong criminal who served thirteen years in prison for the murder of Detroit police detective Russell Blanchard in 1952. In 1965, the state supreme court ruled that there had been an error in Emrick's original trial. He was granted a new trial and pleaded guilty to a reduced charge of manslaughter and was given a sentence of two and a half to fifteen years. He was released after serving the maximum amount of time.

Usiondek and Patros were charged with assault to commit armed robbery. Usiondek was also charged with a second robbery and sentenced to twenty-five to thirty years in prison. In 1973, Usionek appealed his sentence and got it reduced. He was released in February 1974 but was sent back to jail on a parole violation and was released again in 1978.

He took his final bow in July 1980, with a murder that rocked the whole city of Hamtramck, much as the killing of Peter Kubert did twenty-eight years earlier.

It was about 6:00 p.m. on Saturday, July 26, 1980, when Usiondek approached Roy Ficaro and his wife Carmella, who were closing their store, Roy's Market, on Jos. Campau Avenue near Caniff Street. Usiondek spoke with Ficaro, convincing him to reopen the store. A short time later, the men came from a back room, where, apparently, they had been arguing. Without warning, Usiondek pulled a gun and shot Ficaro. He then turned and ran across the street and to an alley, where he fired at a woman who had turned her car into the alley. She was hit but survived the attack. Within minutes of the initial shooting, Hamtramck police were swarming through the area.

Roman Usiondek committed his last crime at Roy's Market on Jos. Campau Avenue near Caniff Street, where he shot owner Roy Ficaro in 1980. Minutes later, he was dead too.

Usiondek's last stand. He took his own life in this area shortly after committing his final murder.

Usiondek ran across the street to the St. Ladislaus Church convent parking lot, apparently not realizing that it was a dead end. He stopped, and maybe took a moment to reevaluate his life, for he turned his .38-caliber up to his head and pulled the trigger.

Police didn't know who he was at first. And the only thing he had was a key to the door of a rooming house in Hamtramck. That's was five decades of crime amounted to. His legacy was summed up twenty-seven years earlier, when he was described by one of his fellow escapees from Jackson prison: "He was a crazy man."

CASE NO. 1942-2

Homicide

Sometimes you might think bartenders have targets painted on their backs. So many of them have been shot through the years that it was often an occupational hazard. But look at their working environment: a combination of alcohol, guns and money. That can easily become a deadly mix. Bartenders also have to contend with what can become an irrational mix of customers. They might start out as civilized, even meek, persons when they order that first drink, but further into the night, they might acquire the personalities of monsters. And the deeper they get into their drinks, the darker their mood might become. Even a sober friend can turn into a drunken mortal enemy. And perhaps even worse, a victim of someone's overindulgence might be totally innocent.

Consider Joseph Lewinski, fifty-four, of 11501 Dequindre Street. He operated a bar just a short distance away at Dequindre and Woodland Streets. At 1:30 a.m. on Monday, April 6, 1942, Lewinski came between a shotgun that was being aimed at Tom Hall, forty-three, and his friend Howard Baker. The result was fatal to Lewinski.

Police said that Hall and Baker were friends who had a falling out that turned physical after a night of drinking. The fight took place about a block from Lewinski's bar. Baker supposedly pulled a knife and cut Hall on the arm. The two separated, with Baker going over to Lewinski's bar. Hall went home and retrieved a shotgun. He went to Lewinski's bar and entered with the shotgun. He spotted Baker and raised the shotgun, looking for Baker. The other twenty-five or so patrons in the bar began to yell, and Lewinski came out from behind the bar. At the same moment, Baker saw Lewinski, and with the timing of an acrobat, Baker ducked, Hall fired and Lewinski stepped into the path of the shotgun blast. He was killed on the spot.

Hall was arrested and charged with first-degree murder. Lewinski was buried.

Case No. 1944-1

Homicide

There was no question about Peter Zuravie's guilt. He understood the seriousness of his crime, and he wasn't afraid to admit it.

"I knew what I was doing," he said when charged with slashing his wife's throat with a pocketknife. He showed no remorse as he pleaded guilty to first-degree murder before Justice of the Peace Thaddeus Machrowicz on January 8, 1944, in Hamtramck court. He was remanded to Wayne County Circuit Court for sentencing.

Just days before, Zuravie, fifty-six, had murdered his wife, Dominica, fifty-five, in the kitchen of their house on Smith Street. He was in his bedroom changing from his bloody clothes when police arrived. They found Dominica lying in a pool of blood when they arrived.

Zuravie told police that his wife had accused him of being drunk when he came home and said she was going to throw a flatiron at him.

Their sixteen-year-old son, Joseph, arrived home shortly after the murder and told his father, "They better keep you a long time because if you get out it will be too bad." Take that for what you will. Another son was in the army serving in New Guinea. A daughter was with her husband, an army private, who was at Fort Still, Oklahoma.

Zuravie was committed to Ionia State Hospital for the Criminally Insane by circuit court judge Thomas J Murphy after he was examined by psychiatrists.

Case No. 1947-1

Homicide

Sometimes the difference between life and death is no more than a few seconds.

Consider Mrs. Stephanie Kawucha, who was gently rocking a two-month-old baby at her Mitchell Street home in July 1947. The calm was broken as she and her common-law husband, Dominic Heretski, began arguing. A neighbor who witnessed the affair told police that Heretski pulled out a knife and stabbed Stephanie. He was arrested a short time later a block away from the crime scene.

Police said Heretski told them, "She told me I was no good and that she never wanted to see me again. Well, she won't see me again...or anybody else."

CASE NO. 1949-1

Homicide

Some murders—and murderers—defy humanity. Such was the case of Stanley Tanski, who shot his ex-wife because she nagged him.

Tanski was arraigned on a charge of first-degree murder in Hamtramck Municipal Court on Friday, May 13, 1949. The arraignment was a formality, as Tanski freely admitted that he shot his ex-wife, Genevieve. Tanski, forty-six, was a train engineer for the Michigan Central Railroad and lived at 2699 Holmes Street. His ex-wife lived with her eight-year-old son, Francis, at 3045 Trowbridge Street, a short walk away.

"I went to her house with a gun wrapped in a newspaper," Tanski told police. "I told her I had a package of pig's knuckles."

The ruse worked, as Genevieve launched into her all-too-familiar litany of rants, demanding alimony from Tanski. He recounted her words: "She said, 'Well, are you going to come across or go to jail?' Then I unwrapped the gun. She got down on her knees in a corner and begged for mercy. But I said, 'No, you're to go. I'm not going to let you get away with anything anymore. Then I shot her, and she fell."

Tanski then walked out of the house and down the street to a bar, where he placed his gun on the counter and told the bartender that he had just killed his wife. Tanski told the bartender to call the police. The bartender picked up the gun and did just that.

6

LAW AND DISORDER

It was a lot easier in the good ol' days.

Back then, if there was trouble, someone would run over to the police station, or what passed for a police station, grab the police chief, and yell, "There's fight down at Charlie Faber's bar. You better get over there before someone gets hurt." The chief would jump on his bicycle and pedal down a dusty or muddy (depending on the weather) Jos. Campau, bust into the bar and clean house, so to speak.

Could that actually have happened? Yeah, but it's hard to say just how many fights there were in the bars around town, although there are references to the early police dragging drunks to the police station because they didn't have a wagon to haul them in. Anytime you mix alcohol and thirsty men, there is bound to be trouble somewhere. But in those days, Hamtramck wasn't known for much of anything, including bar fights. And most of the high-rollers in town were members of the Hamtramck Indians, a group that liked to play hard—that's how they got their name. Folks said they "sounded like a group of wild Indians" (please bear the stereotype; it's a direct quote), and in fact, while they were dedicated to doing good, like raising money for charities, not making a ruckus, they were implicated in some nefarious activities involving alcohol.

That was when the new century—the twentieth century—had just arrived, and Hamtramck was only beginning to feel its growing pains. Before that, Hamtramck was no more than a collection of stores, bars and scattered farms, mainly clustered along and near Jos. Campau Avenue. The massive

... Cut Shows Shipman's Subdivision as it is Today. One Year Ago it was a Dairy Farm. Now we have Cement Walks, Water, Shade Trees, and Sewers are being constructed. We Know that this is

POSITIVELY THE BEST

Proposition to Get a Home or a Good Investment

SHIPMAN'S SUBDIVISION

OF THE CARPENTER FARM, HAMTRAMCK

We ask you to come out to the property and believe that you will be more than satisfied.

$250 Buys Lot 60x112 Feet | **$500** Buys Lot 120x112 Feet

Including Water, Sewer, Cement Sidewalks and Shade Trees.

$5.00 Down, $5.00 Per Month Secures One of These Lots. 5% Discount for Cash

You have no interest or taxes to pay for one year. Thereafter 5 per cent on the unpaid balance. This property is free and clear. Union Trust Guaranteed Abstract given with each lot.

A BUILDING PROPOSITION UNEQUALED ONLY $100.00 down on any lot, and we furnish you money to build your HOME. Pay it back like rent.

DON'T WAIT. To delay is a mistake. The lots are going fast. Many lots were sold last week. If your home is on this Subdivision and you are employed in the vicinity of the Milwaukee Junction district you can walk to and from your business. Just think what this means to you in the saving of car fare in one year.

Several houses have already been erected and are now occupied; others are going up rapidly, so you will have good neighbors all around you.

Agents on the ground afternoons and all day Sunday. Take Chene street car to Railroad crossing, then look for the BIG SIGN directing you to the property.

UNDERWOOD & INNIS 411 Union Trust Bldg.
MAIN 85.

To maximize use of the space available and the influx of immigrants, land developers crowded houses onto small lots. Often, multiple families occupied the houses, leading to tremendous overcrowding.

influx of immigrants in town didn't start to take place until after 1910, when the Dodge Main factory opened.

In the early 1910s, Barney Whalen, his two deputies and his bicycle made up the whole Hamtramck Police Department, and apparently, that was enough. But with the rapid population growth due to the Dodge factory and nearly two dozen other manufacturing plants that opened in town, Hamtramck's new character was forged over the space of a few years. While the growth brought prosperity to the town, it also created tremendous disruption. Vacant land and fields were platted into streets with lots drawn to define spaces for houses. Whole neighborhoods seemed to appear overnight as land speculators and investors grabbed up as much property as they could. Real estate in Hamtramck suddenly became extremely valuable.

With people came problems. Like the town itself, the demands and requirements of a major community expanded. Sewers and water lines needed to be installed, and roads needed paving. There were no parks or recreational spaces for kids or adults, and reasonable zoning wasn't considered. Everything was mashed together. Even today, the buildings that once housed small factories, a brewery and other businesses can be found nesting among blocks of houses. The factories were built in neighborhoods and houses were built within feet of factory walls so that employees could walk to work. It seemed like a good idea at the time, and it was, provided you didn't mind smoking chimneys, clanging steel presses and all the other smells and sounds produced by the factories all through the day and night.

Then there was the human condition to consider. Cram a lot of people together, and sooner or later, you are going to have trouble. People got drunk and got into fights. Drunks stumbling home from the bars at night were easy targets for thieves. And as the number of people grew, so did the pressures and intensity of close-quarter town living. Hardly anybody bothered with the feed store on Jos. Campau Avenue when the area was basically farmland. But when banks started appearing all over town, they proved to be attractive targets for robbers. When Prohibition arrived in 1919, the social fabric of Hamtramck was shredded.

Like the town itself, the Hamtramck Police Department was slow to respond to the rapid changes. That could be blamed on the village council. It was utterly overwhelmed by the changes taking place all over town and seemingly could not react properly. The members just didn't know what to do. It's one thing to govern a village of five hundred people; it's quite another to direct a town of twenty thousand, which is about how large Hamtramck had grown by 1915. And it's still another thing altogether when the town leaders don't like the majority of people who make up this swelling population. Remember, Hamtramck at this period was lorded over by the remnants of the German farmers who had settled there in the nineteenth century. The new arrivals were Poles, who were traditionally enemies of the Germans in Europe. So, not only did the Germans in control not do a lot to accommodate the new residents, but they also didn't have any incentive to accommodate them. In fact, they bitterly, albeit peacefully, fought against them. Eventually, the sheer weight of numbers made the difference, as the

In 1915, the Hamtramck Police Department consisted of (*front row, from left*) Chief Barney Whalen and Daniel O'Brien and (*back row, from left*) Mark Berlinger, Earl Thompson and John Ferguson. Note the wooden sidewalk beneath their feet.

Poles wrested political power from the Germans. But crime doesn't know nationalities. Poles robbed Poles and stole from them regardless of their common heritage. They even killed each other, as we see on these pages. And clearly, as the population grew, so did the need for a large, modern, efficient police department.

Police records from the 1910s are surprisingly scarce. There is a group photo taken in about 1915 capturing the image of a half-dozen officers who made up the entire department. Barney Whalen was chief. He became its first chief in 1913 and served until 1920, when he was succeeded by Fred Dibble. But Whalen is not forgotten, even though almost nobody today knows who he was. Whalen Street is named after him. In 1915, the department found a permanent home in the new village hall that had just been constructed on Jos. Campau Avenue at Grayling Street. Before that, the police station was housed in a small building at Denton and McDougall Streets.

While a detective bureau had been established before 1920, it appears that it didn't keep many records. By the time Hamtramck Village became a city in 1922, it must have been clear that the department needed to enter the twentieth century, although a bit late, and grow with the times. The detective bureau was joined by a traffic division. Initially, the traffic division did nothing but provide officers to direct traffic. But as Hamtramck developed into a metropolitan community, traffic became a major concern. While the number of fatal car accidents in the city hovered at about 12 between 1927 and 1929, the number of nonfatal accidents shot up from 721 to 997. The number of children injured and killed also increased, mainly from kids running into the street and being struck by passing cars. With few playgrounds in town, kids often resorted to playing in the streets, often darting out from in between parked cars. So, along with directing traffic, the division took on the responsibilities of investigating accidents and keeping records of traffic tickets. The department became so important that it was given its own quarters in Village Hall.

By 1926, the division also established an auto drivers' school, which had an attendance of 1,111 novice drivers (822 passed their driver's exam). Additionally, an auto squad was formed just to investigate auto thefts, which to this day has been a particularly persistent problem for Hamtramck. During 1926, some 408 cars were stolen in Hamtramck. Of those, 372 were recovered.

In 1924, the police department took another significant step forward by establishing a women's division. Susan Glinsky was loaned to Hamtramck by the Detroit police to help start the division. She spent a year organizing the department before turning it over to A.R. Paul and Glinsky's assistant, Sophie Stawicki.

It's clear that by the late 1920s Hamtramck had a sophisticated police department that while certainly not as large as the Detroit Police Department was in the same league of professionalism. But even as the department grew

Village Hall was built in 1914 and housed the police department, fire department, village council chambers and village offices. It's the closest thing Hamtramck has ever had to a real city hall.

As Hamtramck grew, so did its police department, which became more sophisticated. Women officers and Black detectives were on staff long before that became common in other towns.

and developed professionally, its base began to rot. Corruption on a host of levels was undermining the department and, in fact, the entire city. The cause was easy to identify: Prohibition. Although well intentioned, this social nightmare achieved far more evil than good. Prohibition was nothing new. There had been movements in America since colonial times to limit the flow of alcohol. People simply drank too much. Often, it was safer to drink alcoholic beverages because water sources were contaminated. And the consumption of alcohol is as old as mankind. By the time Prohibition was implemented nationally in 1920, Hamtramck had a population of about forty-eight thousand people and about 83 percent of them were Polish Catholics. The heart of the most sacred Catholic ceremony, the Mass, includes the drinking of wine. Not grape juice or nonalcoholic wine, but genuine wine (some exceptions are now made). So, to tell the Poles that drinking was immoral was absurd. And the thinking was that if it's not immoral, it shouldn't be illegal. Soon, speakeasies and stills were everywhere. People brewed beer and gin in their bathrooms, attics, basements and barns. There are stories of barns located along the alleys, where windows were installed in the back so you could drive up to buy a bottle without having to get out of your car. This innovative approach predated drive-in banking and fast-food restaurants by decades. Such things were illegal, of course, but somehow, they managed to escape the gaze of the police. Well, there was really no mystery to that. The police were being bribed. It would not be proper to say that is understandable but consider the situation. If you were a cop who took a bribe to ignore an illegal still or a speakeasy, you were not subject to scorn. You were doing everyone a favor by allowing people to buy what they felt should be legally available to them. You weren't corrupt (at least not too much). You were reasonable.

Sometimes, police officers got too chummy with the public. When Prohibition was enacted, many bootleggers took advantage of the familiarity for the sake of cash.

Plus, Hamtramck was in a perfect position. Only five miles from the

Detroit River, which was a highway for illegal booze being shipped in from Canada, it was a sanctuary where thirsty Detroit politicians and police officials could come for a quiet drink out of the spotlight of the big city. For the cop walking a beat to the police official to the mayor of the city, the temptation was just too great. There was money to be made by not doing anything, although sometimes you had to pass along a warning to the local speakeasy that a raid was being planned.

In spite of the widespread corruption, the police did maintain a veneer of attention to Prohibition. The department had "clean-up squads," whose function was to deal with vice of all kinds. Periodically, the mayor at the time would pronounce that conditions in Hamtramck were deplorable and disgraceful and there would be an immediate crackdown on vice. Raids would be conducted, stills smashed and even a few people sent to prison. But there's a new headline every day, and once the big news grew stale, so did showcase raids. And the stills and speakeasies were soon back in operation with barely a hiccup in production.

This is how Hamtramck developed such a bad reputation across the country. National newspapers and magazines wrote about conditions in Hamtramck, portraying the city as virtually lawless. And to an extent they were right. Conditions were, indeed, abominable. In 1923, the Michigan State Police assumed control of the Hamtramck Police Department and conducted a series of more than one hundred raids of places in the city. But their efforts were thwarted by the local police, who continued to alert the targets of the raids. Eventually, even the state police gave up and left.

A case can be made for justifying, or at least understanding, the widespread tolerance for liquor, but the illicit activities that accompanied it are harder to explain away. Drug use and juvenile delinquency skyrocketed during this period, and houses of prostitution flourished. The situation became so bad that mothers were afraid to let their children play outside because the women were enticing them.

The end of Prohibition helped counter the moral decline in town, but the bad behavior by so many was engrained in the community. The moms were largely successful in clearing out the whorehouses, but there were local hotels, and much later the infamous Berkshire Inn motel across from the Dodge Main plant, that operated as brothels well into the 1970s. The same was true for alcohol. The speakeasies closed after Prohibition ended, and bars became legal. Patrick "Paddy" McGraw, perhaps Hamtramck's most legendary whorehouse/speakeasy operator, closed his infamous house of ill repute soon after the end of Prohibition.

The public destruction of slot machines by the police in 1929 was a community event. But there were plenty more of the devices around town.

"Too much competition," he said. But even as legally operating bars flourished in Hamtramck, illegal stills were periodically uncovered in town for decades to come. So was a seemingly endless assortment of gambling operations. These became part of the culture of Hamtramck. You could go to any number of bling pigs in town, where you could shoot craps or play poker, but even more common were "mutuels," a form of numbers betting that pooled bets with winners determined by an assortment of numbers drawn from various sources, such as the amount bet on horse races or even stock market figures. Slot machines were also surprisingly popular, especially in bars.

"Council Orders Drive on Gambling devices," a two-deck banner headline proclaimed on the front page of the *New Deal* newspaper on November 30, 1939. The story noted, "Aiming his attack squarely at the spread of slot machines, Councilman Joseph T. Kuberacki, in a unanimously supported Council resolution Tuesday night ordered the police department to take immediate action in eliminating all forms of gambling devices.

"'There are hundreds of these…in Hamtramck and it's time we got rid of them,'" Kuberacki said.

This kind of pronouncement was regularly made by one city official or another through the 1930s, and they achieved almost nothing. Raids were conducted and machines confiscated, and in short order, they were back in operation. It became routine. In fact, all forms of corruption became tolerated if not openly accepted.

That was almost a fatal problem. But as it turned out, it wasn't the worst evil to befall the city. Even more insidious was the culture of corruption that became so common that it was standard operating procedure. The roots can be traced to the original city charter adopted when Hamtramck village incorporated as a city in 1922. The demon can be found there, innocuously, on page 64 in chapter 8, Pensions for Firemen and Policemen.

Section 1 reads: "Any person who has served as a member of the fire or police force of the City of Hamtramck for a period of twenty-five years, and the time of service on such force in the Village of Hamtramck shall be included in such period of twenty-five years, or any such fireman or policeman who may subsequent to the adoption of this Charter, be disabled in the discharge of his duties as such fireman or policeman shall be placed on the list of retired firemen or policemen."

Section 2 continues: "Any member who retires shall be paid at the rate of one-half of the pay of the rank in which such member was serving at the time of retirement and, in the event of change at any time thereafter, in said rate of pay, then at the rate of one-half the pay for said rank so changed."

The killer was the first sentence in Section 2: "Any member who retires shall be paid at a rate on one-half of the pay of the rank in which such member was serving at the time of retirement." That laid the foundation for financial disaster. Consider that a firefighter could join the force at age twenty, work for twenty-five years and retire at age forty-five, a relatively young age to retire in any profession. But then the retiree would receive half pay for the rest of his or her life, conceivably forty more years. And should the firefighter die, his or her spouse would continue to receive the pension, extending the obligation even longer. Another huge flaw was the stipulation that the retiree was paid based on the rate being paid when the person retired. So, it became common for firefighters and police officers to be promoted just before they retired so that they could collect a higher pension.

And how was this generosity to be covered? The city charter provides that "all fines imposed upon members of the fire and police force for violation of rules, shall be paid into the City Treasury (to cover pension costs)." One can only imagine how much money that raised, but it couldn't have amounted to much. The pension system was revised in 1938 to have the employees make contributions to the pension system from their salary. But by then the damage had been done. It was becoming evident that the city could not support such a system, yet the politicians did what politicians are best at doing, namely, nothing. They kicked the problem down the road for the next generation to deal with.

What mattered to many was what they could get then. Prohibition was a huge motivator in that respect. Two mayors, Peter Jezewski and Rudolph Tenerowicz, drew prison sentences for their involvement in illegal Prohibition activities, and they both were treated like royalty by the local population. So, what incentive was there for the cop walking the beat who is struggling to support his family to refuse a little bribe? Nothing much, just look the other way when the truck loaded with liquor pulls into the garage down the street. Or don't go down the street where the blind pig is operating. Or don't do both of those things, and the next day, add another one to the list and then another. Even after Prohibition, gambling, prostitution and vices of all sorts thrived. And the whole social structure of Hamtramck cracked under the pressure. But that is not to say that no one cared. Many good Hamtramckans were ashamed about what was happening and began to take action. We've already mentioned the moms wielding broomsticks to drive the prostitutes out of town. But others were taking a more measured approach to deal with the fundamental problems of the city.

In 1941, the Michigan Municipal League did a comprehensive study of the city, titled Financial Administrative Survey of the City of Hamtramck, Michigan. Included in it was a hard-hitting examination of the city's police department. The first paragraph set the tone for what was to follow:

The main duties of a municipal police department are to protect life and property, by preventing the occurrence of offenses and accidents, maintain order, apprehend criminals and to reduce losses by making recoveries of stolen property. To discharges its duties effectively, the department must have competent leadership, carefully selected and well-trained personnel, proper organization, workable procedures for handling police operations, and adequate equipment which is well maintained. The Hamtramck police department is almost totally lacking in nearly all these essentials. It has no real head, continuity of leadership and lacks forceful direction; its personnel is not selected with regard for adaptability to police work and is untrained;

its organization is not clean cut and lines of authority are not followed; and its methods are far from modern. Only in equipment is it reasonably well prepared for its job.

And that was only the beginning. The next twenty pages of the report dissected the department. Comments like this were common: "There is no training. New recruits are placed with older officers to 'break them in' and after that they are required to shift for themselves. No attempt is made to retrain the older members of the department in the more modern police policies."

The report also specifically proposed a new Vice Division, which would operate independently from the detective bureau and report directly to the chief of police.

How much of this was actually adopted by the department is difficult to assess from a viewpoint nearly eighty years later, but clearly, it was recognized that changes had to be made, and they had to extend beyond the police department. In 1942, a dramatic shift in attitude was expressed by the people of Hamtramck. They elected Dr. Stephen Skrzycki as mayor. He vowed to clean up Hamtramck, but unlike his predecessors, who made such vows routinely, he meant it. And the 1940s marked a period when vice and all its trappings withered. It would never be eliminated. Even into the 1970s, illegal stills were being uncovered and prostitution remained a problem. But it was nothing to the degree of the 1920s and '30s. The outbreak of World War II had an impact. Many of the young men were drafted, and from time to time, the courts would offer young nonviolent offenders the choice of going to jail or joining the army. In time, Hamtramck buried its past to such a degree that many of the old-time politicians, places and events were totally forgotten. And anyone who was curious about Hamtramck's past was discouraged from looking into it. Unfortunately, for every Vice King Chester LaMare there was a brilliant and innovative educator like Maurice Keyworth who was buried in the sands of time.

In Memoriam
Dr. M. R. Keyworth
Superintendent of Hamtramck Public Schools 1923-1935; State Superintendent of Public Instruction, Elect 1935. Died June 22, 1935

Maurice Keyworth brought national recognition to Hamtramck for his innovative education policies, yet he is largely forgotten today.

So, what does this mean? It was the Hamtramck police who were charged with keeping order and solving murders, and they did—to varying degrees, given the challenges, temptations and hurdles they had to overcome to keep the town from slipping into total chaos. Again, they did that to varying degrees.

Today, murder investigations are far more complex and comprehensive, and it would be a great disservice to the police department to imply by omission that it has not advanced with the years. Reports of corruption are virtually unheard of in Hamtramck now. Murders still occur but are much rarer than they were even in the 1970s. Today's police in Hamtramck have to deal with some different issues, such as working with an incredibly diverse population. Languages barriers and different customs pose special challenges for the police.

But like the city as a whole, they have adapted and grown.

POLICE CASE NO. 1

Herman Schmidt—Killed in the Line of Duty

It was a frozen day in February 1917, when Officer Herman Schmidt was gunned in sight of the old police station at Jos. Campau and Grayling Streets, ushering in an investigation that would find new life twenty-six years after the fatal shots were fired.

It began as a prank. A group of boys started it by throwing snowballs at two men who were walking on Jos. Campau. The men confronted the boys. One of the men began arguing with the boys, and a brief fight broke out.

A witness said that one of the men swung at a youth, missed and fell to the ground. As he rose, he pulled a gun and began shooting. Three youths, aged eleven, thirteen and fourteen, and a man aged twenty, were all hit. It isn't known how seriously they were injured. Old police records note, "Not expected to live," but there are no further records of them. Interestingly, one of the boys hit was the son of the Hamtramck police chief.

Officer Schmidt was in the police station at the time, and hearing gunshots, he ran outside and began chasing one of the two men. Schmidt might not have known that he was chasing the gunman. The other man ran in a different direction and disappeared. Schmidt chased the other man down the block, until the man slipped behind a utility pole and fired at Schmidt, hitting him in the chest. Then the gunman also disappeared. In March, police arrested a twenty-three-year-old machinist named Michael Monahan, who lived in Hamtramck. But evidently their case didn't stick.

The investigation went nowhere from there, and the case slipped into history. Years passed. Then, in August 1943, police received a tip leading them to reopen the investigation. Incredibly, they were able to find some of the original witnesses, as well as the man implicated in the shooting. However, he denied any involvement in the shooting and said he had never heard of Schmidt. The police placed the man in a lineup, but none of the witnesses were able to identify him. So, he was released. And the case of who shot Herman Schmidt remains open to this day.

POLICE CASE No. 2

John T. Mickley—Killed in the Line of Duty

It's a cruel thought, but every day a police officer goes to work could be his or her last. Circumstances can change in a moment from routine boredom to a life or death situation. And it doesn't always end well. Such was the case of officer John T. Mickley, who was patrolling Jos. Campau Avenue and Caniff Street with Detective Lieutenant John Rustoni at about 10:30 p.m. on September 1, 1930.

They came upon John Witkowski in the process of robbing Frank Strukel by the night deposit box at the Bank of Hamtramck (later known as First State Bank). Strukel was depositing the day's receipts from the Martha Washington Theater, which was just across the street from the bank. Witkowski saw the officers and opened fire on their scout car and then ran into the Mitchell Street alley, around the corner from the bank. Mickley exited the car and chased Witkowski, catching up with him at Casmere Street and wresting Witkowski's handgun away from him. As Mickley was leading Witkowski to the police car, Witkowski pulled away. Mickley shot him, hitting him in the hip. But Witkowski didn't go down. He jumped at Mickley, grabbing the gun.

Peter Pleva, who lived nearby, saw the fight from his house. He told police, "The bandit grabbed Mickley's wrist. He kept the officer's hand containing the pistol at an angle away from his body. The two wrestled

Frank Strukel walked from Martha Washington Theater (*right*) to the bank across the street (*left*), where he was by John Witkowski and not far from where Witkowski shot and killed police officer John Mickley.

back and forth. Mickley's gun went off six times during the battle, but the shots went into the air. Then the bandit broke loose and shot twice. Both bullets hit Mickley in the neck. He dropped. The bandit ran across the street and down another alley."

Rustoni heard the shots and rushed to the site and found Mickley dying. Help was called, and Mickley was transported to Hamtramck Municipal Hospital, which later became known as St. Francis Hospital. But Mickley died on the way.

Six days later, Witkowski was arrested at his girlfriend's house in Detroit. Witkowski was tried and convicted of murder. He was sentenced to life in prison in solitary confinement at Marquette Prison. He died in prison on December 15, 1963.

Mickley was survived by his wife and a stepdaughter. Originally from Michigan City, Indiana, Mickley served as a security officer for Michigan Central Railroad before he joined the Hamtramck Police Department.

POLICE CASE NO. 3

Frank Boza—Killed in the Line of Duty

Frank Boza joined the ranks of a handful of Hamtramck police officers who gave their lives for the law on March 4, 1924. Boza was at the police station

Police officer Frank Boza was shot near this bank, which was just across the street from the police station.

working the front desk when a holdup alarm went off at People's National Bank at Jos. Campau Avenue and Council Street. That was just a short way down the block from the police station, which at that time was at Jos. Campau Avenue and Grayling Street in the old village hall.

A gang of clever thieves set off an alarm at the north end of town to draw the police away from the bank, which was at the South End of town. Plus, they might have thought the police would be skeptical of an alarm across the street from the police station. In any case, the gang entered the bank with guns drawn.

As soon as the alarm sounded, officers led by Sergeant Boza and Detective Sergeant John Sitkorski raced from the police station and ran across the street to the bank. One of the robbers, John Tremenaro, acted as lookout and saw the officers running toward them. Tremenaro began shooting. Boza returned fire, and bullets flew back and forth. But then Boza was hit in the neck. Sitkorski fired and hit Tremenaro in the heart and arm, mortally wounding him. A second robber fled from the bank and down a nearby street to the Michigan Central Railroad yard, where he was cornered by police and arrested. Sergeant Boza walked back to the police station, where he collapsed. He was taken to Grace Hospital in Detroit, and he died two hours later. He was thirty-two years old and left a wife and three children

7

THOSE NOT-SO-GOLDEN YEARS

Hamtramck isn't what it used to be.

You hear that a lot as we move further into the twenty-first century. Invariably, those who say that remember Hamtramck in its "Golden Years," the 1950s and '60s, when they likely were growing up in town. Hamtramck was a fabulous place to grow up. While it lacked the more modern amenities of wealthier cities, it made up for that with street-side opportunities that were more exciting than a fancy playground. You couldn't beat racing your bike through the bush-lined curving walkways around Hamtramck High School, even if you did crash into a brick wall every so often. And no bike rider wore a helmet.

They also remember Jos. Campau Avenue when it was at its busiest. It was packed with stores that lined both sides of the street. Sure, there were other major streets in town, like Conant Avenue and Caniff and Holbrook Streets, but Jos. Campau was where the action was. It formed a canyon from one end of town to the other, where you could find every type of store imaginable. There was Max's jewelry store, Federals department store, Witkowski's clothing store, Helen's Toyland, Wonder Bazaar with its religious goods, Pure Foods supermarkets and the dime stores, Kresge's, Grant's and Neisner's. And don't forget Sweetlands's or Delis' ice cream parlors. Mixed among them were Martha Washington and Farnum Theaters, which were the only movie houses that survived the onslaught of television in the late 1940s. Prior to that, you could also count Campau, Pasttime, White Star and even Jewell Theaters (if you want to go back to 1912) in the movie house mix.

Jos. Campau Avenue is the touchstone to the nostalgia most longtime and former Hamtramckans feel today. The schools and neighborhood streets figure into the mix too. But Jos. Campau Avenue, with its lights and action, made the biggest impression. Where else could a ten-year-old boy buy a plastic model airplane kit for twenty-nine cents? Even in one of mom's tightest weeks, she could manage to squeeze an extra quarter and nickel from the bottom of her purse.

On Friday evenings, Saturdays and Sundays, the sidewalks of Jos. Campau Avenue were packed with so many shoppers that it was difficult to maneuver among them. It's no surprise that from the 1920s to the 1960s Jos. Campau Avenue actually rivaled downtown Detroit as the busiest shopping district in southeast Michigan.

Today, Jos. Campau Avenue is still a viable shopping district, but it is a shadow of what it was. All those dime stores and department stores are long gone. And few can even remember where Sweetland's was located. The proliferation of suburban shopping malls in the 1960s and 1970s, combined with the population exodus, tore the heart out of Jos. Campau Avenue. And that was followed by the rise of the internet, which dampened any resurgence of neighborhood stores. Ironically, many of the shopping malls are now fighting for their lives, and some have already lost the battle to shopping online. But Jos. Campau Avenue endures. A little more ragged and whole lot older but still alive. So, in a sense, those who pine for the past are correct. Hamtramck is not what it used to be. But then again, neither are any of us. And really if you dare delve into the past—not just what you remember or misremember—you will find that it never was quite what we think it was. The difference is the distinction between nostalgia and history. Nostalgia is fondly recalling when you were a kid in the springtime, and they canceled school and you got to play baseball all week in the streets, and it was so much fun that it seemed like a dream. History is knowing that they closed the schools for several days because two kids died of polio that week, and it was too dangerous to keep the schools open. That actually happened. The wonderful old wading pool at the corner of Holbrook Street and Conant Avenue was closed and filled with dirt in the early 1950s because it was thought to be a breeding ground for polio.

And the balloon deflating images go on and on from there. For every story that appeared in the local newspaper about a new product being produced at Dodge Main, there is another one about the plant seeking a tax cut or threatening to close or dealing with another strike. This occurred routinely throughout the 1950s and 1960s.

Closing schools during a pandemic is not a new concept. In August 1939, the Hamtramck School Board decided to postpone the opening of the new school year because of the threat of polio. That happened a number of times before the disease was finally contained.

The city's finances, which had been a fiscal train wreck since 1922, took on traumatic proportions in the 1950s, thanks to a variety of factors, including the bloated pension system. Mayor Albert Zak, who was a shrewd politician and a competent administrator, raised the alarm as the threat of payless paydays for employees became a reality. But no one else in city government seemed interested in the looming crisis. The year 1959 was a watershed, of sorts. The city was deluged by a host of financial problems.

The June 11, 1959 lead story in the *Hamtramck Citizen* newspaper captured the situation quite well: "City Financial Outlook Bleak. Hamtramck's municipal financial outlook was at its lowest point this week when the machinery started grinding away on the Chrysler Corporation's appeal for a 75% cut on its Hamtramck properties....

"To make matters even bluer, the city's some 400 workers went without their paychecks yesterday for the first time in years....And it will take some fancy maneuvering plus an overdose of good luck for the workers to get their checks on July 30, 1959."

That was followed by a string of equally chilling stories in the *Citizen*:

City Water Deficit $108,848
May lease system to Detroit Board

Operations of the department in the fiscal year cost $518,635. Receipts totaled but $409,787 of which $363,628 was for sale of water, $158 was the balance at the beginning of the fiscal year and $46,000 borrowed from the general fund.

And on October 29, 1959, came a bombshell: "An atomic bomb could hardly have caused much more confusion in Hamtramck City Hall this week than did the news of the city's loss of one-sixth of its tax income in one sweeping decision by the State Tax Commission. In round figures, the Chrysler assessment of $49 million was trimmed to the depression level of $29 million, and the city's tax base shriveled to what it was a decade ago," the *Citizen* reported.

Mayor Albert Zak recognized that Hamtramck's financial base was crumbling in the 1950s. Faced with an uncooperative city council, there was little he could do about it. But he did understand the need to have top-quality equipment.

In city hall the gloom was heavier than elsewhere because if anyone stood lose more it was the city employees.

Mayor Zak declared a state of emergency with a ten-point austerity program. It included a hiring freeze, laying off all part-time employees and mandatory retirement of all employees age sixty-five and over, among other measures. When the Chrysler tax cut was announced, the common council had nothing to say. At a council meeting that lasted all of four minutes, no one mentioned the financial crisis. The city appealed the cutback and won a partial victory in early 1960. But the mold was set. Through the 1960s, the city would fight similar battles. One day, the Dodge Main factory was held up as the symbol of prosperity, goodness and a mechanical representation of heaven on earth. The next day, it was nothing more than a thieving den of blind capitalists whose main purpose of being was to destroy Hamtramck.

This hardly seems like the stuff of a golden age.

The greatest irony is that when Dodge Main did close in 1979, long after the golden age ended, Hamtramck somehow found the strength to persevere.

Meanwhile, on the sometimes mean streets of Hamtramck, stories of murders kept taking up space in the local newspapers.

CASE NO. 1953-1

Homicide

All kinds of factors can play into the causes of murder, but perhaps one of the most fundamental is the one that is likely as old as humanity: jealousy. No, not the feeling of inadequacy because you neighbor has a nicer house, but the one that tears at the heart.

That's what led to the tragedy of Robert and Mary Magers. Mary was thirty-nine and Robert was thirty-six when they died in April 1953. They lived in an upper flat at 2229 Faber on the city's south side. But they didn't live well. They frequently quarreled; Robert was known as a heavy drinker and was extremely jealous of his wife. It was a deadly combination.

At about 1:00 a.m. on Tuesday, April 21, 1953, Arthur and Mary Jurkowski, who lived in the flat below the Magers, were awakened by the sound of two gunshots. They called police. Detectives Ted Rodgers and Val Walker arrived about twenty minutes later. They went upstairs and forced the door of the Magerses' apartment. There they found Mary on the floor. She had been shot in the forehead. John was nearby. He, too, had been shot in the forehead. A .22-caliber rifle rested between his knees, pointing toward his heart. Apparently, he had shot her and then turned the gun on himself. John had borrowed the gun from a coworker at Chevrolet Gear and Axle plant just a few blocks from their home. Going through the apartment, police found signs of domestic problems, including a heartbreaking letter Mary had written to her husband. "I care more for you than you know," she wrote, "and there might be a future for us."

She suggested they meet and talk. She, along with their son and daughter, had left the apartment a week earlier, Arthur Jurkowski told police.

Case 1954-1

Homicide (Justifiable)

Appearances certainly can be deceiving. It looked like David Solomon, thirty-nine, shot and killed Howard Flowers, twenty-seven, in August 1954, and indeed he did. But as it turned out, he had a reason.

The shooting happened at about 10:15 p.m. on Sunday, August 15, at Solomon's house at 2231 Newton, a street that disappeared years ago on the far south side of town. That evening, Flowers, his brother Rollins and three other men came to Solomon's house, where a conversation turned into an argument in the backyard.

Suddenly, Solomon ran into the house. He was pursued by two of the men, and in the confusion, Flowers was shot. Witnesses said they saw Solomon run from the house with a gun in his hand. Flowers was taken to Receiving Hospital in Detroit, where he died about eight hours later. Solomon went into hiding but soon gave himself up to police.

Solomon was questioned by an assistant prosecuting attorney. Solomon claimed the shooting was self-defense, and the prosecuting attorney agreed. The shooting was ruled as justifiable homicide.

CASE NO. 1954-2

Homicide/Robbery

Where is Sherlock Holmes when you need him?

Perhaps even that mighty detective would have been baffled by the case of John J. Jurewicz, forty-nine, of 2259 Bernard Street. It's believed that he was murdered on the night of March 3, 1954, although the exact time might differ, as his body was in a snow-covered car for as much as a day after.

For twenty years, Jurewicz had been a salesman at the Quaker Produce Co. at 3303 Caniff Street. Shortly before 6:00 p.m. on March 3, he left his office and headed to a local bank to make a night deposit of $4,852 in checks. At around 6:00 p.m., police were called to the intersection of Caniff and Gallagher Streets by a man who was so excited that the dispatcher transferred his call to the fire department. The man reported that he "saw a man shot in a car" near Caniff and Gallagher. Then he hung up without identifying himself or giving any further information. Police responded, but

It was about here that John Jurewicz's snow-covered car was parked—with his body inside.

it had been snowing, and all of the parked cars were covered with a layer of snow. It was misleadingly serene, and the police, seeing nothing out of place, assumed the caller had heard a car back firing.

Compounding the circumstances, Jurewicz's wife, Sophia, later told them that she last saw her husband at noon on Wednesday, March 3, as he hadn't come home from work in the evening. But that was not unusual, she said. He often spent the night at his brother's house. But when he didn't come home Thursday, she called the brother, who said he hadn't been there. A call to Quaker Produce Co. raised an alarm, since Jurewicz had not reported to work that day, and no one knew where he was. His body was found later that day by Jerome Dudek, owner of the Quaker Company.

Police were called, and at first, it was thought that Jurewicz had died of a heart attack. A postmortem was done at the Wayne County Morgue, where it was discovered that he had been shot with a .38-caliber pistol.

Police immediately stepped up the investigation, trying to identify the caller. But they had no luck there. Several persons were questioned by police, but all had alibis for the time in question. Police had another tip: a two-tone hardtop convertible occupied by "four or five men" was seen in the company parking lot before Jurewicz was killed. Police tracked such a car to Chicago, but the owner was able to prove that he was nowhere near Hamtramck when the murder occurred. So, that tip didn't lead anywhere either.

Finally, police were led to a suspect who had a .38-pistol at a barbershop at 1816 Caniff Street. The man was arrested for having an illegal weapon, but a ballistics test showed that it was not the murder weapon.

Quaker Produce offered a $1,000 reward for information leading to the arrest and conviction of Jurewicz's killer. There's no record of the reward being collected or anyone being arrested.

And the checks were never found.

CASE NO. 1955-1

Homicide/Manslaughter

It was blood dropping from the ceiling onto the women's bathroom floor of the Flying Duck Bar that led to the discovery of the body of Charles L Chinn. And that eventually made legal history by introducing the first taped confession in a murder trial in Michigan.

But the path from the bathroom to the court room proved to be a difficult one to follow.

It started in June 1955, when Mike Chiviges, manager of the Flying Duck Bar at 7735 Jos. Campau Avenue, not far from the massive Dodge Main auto factory, called police about the blood stains. The blood appeared to come from a small catalogue appliance store located above the bar. The one-room store was owned by Charles L. Chinn, forty-eight. Chiviges had first seen the blood on Tuesday and called the building owner. He couldn't reach the owner but left a message. The owner came by the next day, and Chinn's body was found. He had suffered numerous skull fractures, the Wayne County Morgue determined. Because the bar had been closed Saturday, Sunday and Monday, two days had passed before the murder was discovered, so police set off on a trail that was five days old. But there was no shortage of manpower. Seven detectives and three patrolmen were assigned to the case, and it didn't take them long to make progress. They quickly came up with a suspect, when Ike Ewell, twenty-nine, of Pingree Street in Detroit, was spotted driving a car that had been owned by Chinn. Ewell had worked for Chinn and, when questioned by police, had proof that he had bought the car from Chinn. Police questioned Ewell for two days and took him to the state police station in Redford to take a lie detector test.

Ewell failed so thoroughly that police said the test was stopped because the machine's needle was vibrating so hard.

Facing that, Ewell confessed. He said that he and Chinn argued over payment for some work that Ewell had done for him. Chinn had offered to pay him one dollar for work that Ewell said was worth twenty-five to thirty dollars. Ewell said Chinn had kicked him during the argument, and Ewell grabbed a hammer and hit Chinn. Chinn fell to the floor, and Ewell continued to strike him. The attack took place at about 4:15 p.m. on the Saturday before his body was discovered. Chinn was married, but his wife said that it wasn't unusual for him to spend several days at a time at the store, so she wasn't concerned when he failed to come home for a while.

Ewell was arraigned on a charge of murder before Judge Charles Kotulski in Hamtramck court, and Ewell waived examination. The case was transferred to Wayne County Circuit Court, where an attorney was appointed to represent Ewell. At that point, he changed his plea to not guilty.

Ewell went to trial, where one of the prosecution's key components was the presentation of a recording of Ewell describing the murder. It was recorded during the interrogation of Ewell and played over a loudspeaker to the jury. This was the first time a recording was played for a jury in Michigan. It must have been effective. Ewell was convicted of first-degree murder and sentenced to life in prison. That could have brought this story to an end, but there is more. Jump forward to September 1965, when Ewell sought a new trial, claiming his rights had been violated during his interrogation, which lasted for four days after his arrest. Ewell claimed that the Michigan Supreme Court had already ruled that a suspect must be arraigned without undue delay, and four days of interrogation exceeded that. Circuit court judge Edward Piggins said Ewell was entitled to a new trial. Ewell pleaded guilty to a charge of manslaughter, which carried a maximum sentence of fifteen years in prison, which was likely a lot less than life in prison.

Case No. 1956-1

Homicide/Robbery

There was a sense outrage in the murder of James Elder, thirty-five, owner of the Hide-A-Way Bar, 8444 St. Aubin Street. Elder was killed during a robbery on Sunday, March 4, 1956. Robberies, even murders in bars, are not especially unusual, but what triggered the anger was that, apparently, Elder was fully cooperating with the robbers when he was shot in the back.

Police and the press termed the killing as "vicious." They said Elder was preparing to close the bar in the early morning hours that Sunday, when four men who had appeared to be sleeping at their table rose up and announced a "stickup." By that time, most of the patrons had left. Elder was ordered to empty the cash register and turned to comply, when a robber shot him in the back. Elder collapsed, and the robbers attempted to pull him into the bathroom but were unable. Two customers who were still in the bar were ordered to lie in the floor, and one was robbed of ten dollars.

As the robbers fled from the bar with about $200, Elder rose up and chased after them. He produced a gun and fired at them but apparently missed them all.

Elder was taken to St. Francis Hospital and transferred to Detroit Receiving Hospital, where he died.

Police detectives James Raspberry and Edward Page identified two suspects, who were taken into custody for questioning. Police also took the table where the four robbers were sitting, as well as several glasses to recover fingerprints.

But the bloody trail led nowhere for four years. Then, in September 1960, the case was revived. After a long investigation, Detectives Henry Ryan and Edward Page arrested Leonard Chaney Jr., twenty-four, who was already in Jackson Prison on another crime. Also arrested was Philip Green, thirty, who was picked up in his home at 4692 Sixteenth Street in Detroit, and George Edward Forest, twenty-four, who was a prisoner in the Ionia Correctional Facility.

Green made a full statement to police, describing how the robbers met in his house to plan the robbery. Cheney and Green were brought to Hamtramck from prison to face charges and bring the case to a close.

Case No. 1958-1

Homicide/Robbery

John Curtis was not an accomplished criminal, but he sure was a busy one. By the time he was thirty-nine, Hamtramck police had arrested him eight times for crimes ranging from embezzlement to burglary. He had also been arrested in Detroit ten times and once in Cleveland, where he was sent to prison for larceny.

But none of that compared to the murder charge he faced in April 1958, when he admitted to killing real estate dealer Walter Culik, sixty-five, and burying his body in a garbage dump near New Baltimore, Michigan.

Curtis was a caretaker at an apartment building that Culik owned. The two got into an argument in the basement of the apartment building over some work that Curtis had done for which Culik refused to pay. The argument escalated, and Curtis struck Culik with a piece of iron pipe. Curtis placed Culik's body in a cabinet and the next day hired a truck to haul the cabinet to the dump. Culik's body was found two days later by a pair of youths searching for firewood. It didn't take long to trace the crime back to Curtis. He was arrested as he tried to flee from his grandmother's house in Detroit.

Culik was known to carry as much as $2,000.00 at any time, but police found only $0.42 on his body, and his wallet was missing.

Case No. 1958-2

Homicide/Robbery

The hardest murders to solve are those when the killer and victim have no connection other than the crime.

Such was the case of Bernard F. Delinski, fifty-six, who was shot by two men who robbed him in his store at 11444 Jos. Campau in the center of the city's shopping district.

It happened on March 1, 1958, and Delinski was shot seven times in the chest and neck. He was transported to St. Francis Hospital, where he died a short time later. The brazen crime alarmed the other merchants in Hamtramck, who offered a $1,000 reward for the arrest and conviction of the killers.

Police had little to go on other than that they were "youthful." Some two hundred local youths were questioned to no avail.

But since then, nothing.

Case No. 1958-3

Homicides

Not all murders involving Hamtramckans occurred in Hamtramck. And in one case, no one knew for nineteen years that a murder even had been committed.

The suspect was Jack Youngblood, who was thirty-nine years old and sent to prison in 1958 to serve three and a half to ten years for molesting a five-year-old girl. Youngblood was no stranger to prison. He had been the guest of three states before being sentenced in Michigan. One of those prisons was in Nashville, Tennessee, where Youngblood was doing time in 1939.

In 1958, while Youngblood was awaiting sentencing on the molesting charge, a Detroit policewoman read a newspaper story about a skeleton found in the rubble of the Nashville prison as it was being demolished. The skeleton was identified as being once under the skin of an inmate named Paul Payne, who was twenty-one years old when he disappeared in 1939. At the time, officials thought he had escaped. The newspaper article mentioned Youngblood and that he admitted to knowing Payne but denied that he had killed him.

Police suspected Youngblood of the killing because after the skeleton had been discovered other inmates told them that Payne and Youngblood had argued during a dice game and then Youngblood buried Payne under the prison floor.

It was a stretch, but it was enough for the cops to take the story seriously. In any case, Tennessee asked to have Youngblood extradited after he served his time on the morals charge.

CASE NO. 1959-1

Homicide

If there is a rule for living in harmony in Hamtramck, it is "don't fight with your neighbor." That applies everywhere, but it is essential in Hamtramck, where breaking that rule can be the difference between living in peace or facing an eternal feud. And sometimes it can be a matter of life and death.

In Hamtramck, almost all of the houses are on lots thirty feet wide by ninety to one hundred feet deep. That means there is about five feet of space between houses. With that kind of proximity, you can expect to have a close relationship with your neighbors, whether you want to or not. The situation becomes even more challenging in winter, when piles of snow reduce the number of parking spots on the streets. Few people have room for garages, and five feet of space between houses is barely wide enough to squeeze in a driveway. Parking spots in front of houses are highly valued, and after a heavy snowfall, a curious collection of chairs can be found popping up like winter mushrooms in the snow on the street. Take a word of advice: if someone spends hours shoveling what seems like tons of snow to clear a parking spot on the street and then claims and protects it with a chair, do not move the chair. While moving such a snow throne can be risky, there doesn't seem to be any record of anyone dying for doing that.

But there's an even more dangerous form of neighborly contact, which isn't limited to Hamtramck and has proved fatal. These deadly affairs involve romance.

Such was the case of Flenoid Provience, forty-eight, of 2443 Wyandotte Street, who got into a vicious fight with his neighbor Douglas Fantroy Sr., sixty-four, over an alleged affair between Provience's wife and Fantroy.

The altercation took place on an evening in early July 1959, when Provience confronted Fantroy on the street near their houses and exchanged words. This quickly escalated to a physical confrontation as Provience pulled a knife and began slashing at Fantroy. Fantroy collapsed on the street. Neighbors rushed in, put him in a car and drove to St. Francis Hospital, just a handful of blocks away from Wyandotte Street. Fantroy was slashed on the left arm inside the elbow and received puncture wounds in the upper part of his chest. He was treated but died on the operating table.

When police arrived, Fantroy's daughter told them that Provience had accused her father of having an affair with Provience's wife. They found Provience in his house and arrested him. He was taken to St. Francis Hospital for treatment for minor lacerations that he received in the fight.

Police detectives Edward Page and Harold Butler questioned several witnesses. They corroborated what Fantroy's daughter had told them.

Provience was arraigned on a charge of murder the next day.

CASE NO. 1959-2

Homicide

Love gone wrong leading to tragedy is a theme that is probably as old as murder itself. Add an innocent victim, and it becomes worse.

Fred McKinney was the innocent one who did nothing more than jump up off the sofa where he was sleeping when Robert Dine, twenty-seven, smashed through the back door of a flat at 6267 Edwin Street in the early morning hours of February 4, 1959, and shot McKinney with a .32-caliber rifle.

Dine apparently had come to the flat looking for his estranged wife. She had moved in with a Mrs. Kopec, who was also separated from her husband.

According to police, Dine had called Mrs. Kopec earlier and told her to "tell my wife I'm mad and I'm not going to let her get away with anything."

CASE NO. 1965-1

Homicide

If any house in Hamtramck should be haunted, it would be a certain one on the 3000 block of Jacob Street.

The tale begins on March 6, 1965, when the sixty-four-year-old owner of the house decided to clean the attic. It hadn't been touched for years. Among the clutter he encountered, there was a small item wrapped in a copy of the October 16, 1950 edition of the *Detroit Free Press*. As he unwrapped the package, he realized that he was holding the body of a baby. Police were called, and the body was taken to the Wayne County Morgue, where it was determined the baby had been murdered. Death apparently had been caused by suffocation. Remnants of a handkerchief were found stuffed in the throat bones of the skeleton.

The homeowner who made the grisly discovery told police that he had only lived there for two years and rented the house. Police contacted the owner, who told them he had bought the house from a family in 1950. Police detectives John Pietrzak and Peter Supina and policewoman Mary Omela were assigned to the case. Despite the span of years, tracking down a suspect didn't take long. The police went as far back as 1940, looking for who lived in the house, and on that journey, contacts they made implicated Antoinette Zawodny, fifty-four, who was quickly located and arrested at her place of employment in Taylor, Michigan. Zawodny had lived in the house from October 1947 to March 1951.

She was arraigned on a charge of first-degree murder before Judge Walter Paruk in Hamtramck Municipal Court. Police said their investigation indicated that the baby had not been born in the house on Jacob Street.

Zawodny was bound over to circuit court for trial, but Judge Joseph Rashid dismissed the charges. Judge Rashid noted the medical examiner's report, which said it was impossible to determine the cause of death or even ascertain that the baby had been born alive. He said that to bring a homicide charge, the existence of a human being must be proven.

What happened with the bones of the baby isn't specified, although it is likely that they were disposed of by the county.

As for the spirit of the little one…

8

THE SPACED-OUT '70s

If it weren't for the '60s, the '70s wouldn't have happened. Well, they would have, but it wouldn't have been the same. The '60s was a time when American broke loose. The postwar "father knows best," prim, pure white conservatism of the 1950s was finally being shaken off as the nation became more socially aware. The assassination of President John F. Kennedy might have had something to do with it. Not only did it traumatize the nation to a degree probably not seen since the murder of Abraham Lincoln, but it also propelled Lyndon Johnson into the Oval Office. And this Texas country boy defied his image and became a champion for civil rights. He also widely expanded the war in Vietnam. These actions helped reshape the United States in the 1960s. Violence was the common factor. The war was violent by its very nature, and much progress was made on the road toward civil rights through the courts and peaceful demonstrations. That defined Dr. Martin Luther King Jr., one of the nation's towering figures, who advocated peaceful resistance, until he himself was the victim of a bullet. And though it might be uncomfortable to remember, riots were sparked in cities across the nation. Detroit was especially hard hit.

On a hot night in the summer of 1967, a police raid of a suspected blind pig on the city's near west side quickly escalated into a street war. Some 43 people were killed and 467 injured and whole neighborhoods were burned to the ground. It can and has been argued that this was not really a race riot but more of a social rebellion of people who were tired of being oppressed and forced to live in poverty. In any case, the result was that

Detroit was seemingly irreparably damaged and would never be the same. Burned businesses were gone for good, and many that weren't harmed soon closed and moved out of the city. Vast areas of empty lots were left in their wake. But perhaps even worse was the psychological damage done to public perception. Detroit was no longer the Motor City. It was the city that had the big riot. It was a violent place. It wasn't safe to go there anymore. White people were not welcome. Sometimes the smallest details reveal the pictures. Consider the auto worker who occasionally frequented the Detroit blind pigs. He would go after work and stay until the early hours of the morning. Black and White people played side by side. After the riot of 1967, no White players went there anymore. There hadn't been any trouble. But things had changed—things that weren't put into words. They were just felt. White flight kicked into higher gear. Detroit's population began to decrease in the early 1950s, after reaching more than 1.8 million. By 1970, it was 1.5 million, and by 1980, it was 1.2 million. The percentages were more startling. Between 1960 and 1970, Detroit's population declined by 9.3 percent. Between 1970 and 1980, the drop was 20.5 percent. Granted, as the population decreased, the percentage numbers reflected the drop disproportionally. But however you cut the numbers, they were dismal.

The worst numbers were homicides. Detroit recorded a massive 714 murders in 1974. Hamtramck would come nowhere near that, but its murder rate took an upward swing through the decade.

Murder in the Main

Think "Dodge City."

The name is synonymous with gunslingers and shootouts—kind of like Hamtramck during Prohibition. Then add a factory called Dodge Main into the picture, and you have a natural link.

Hamtramck is a city in a city, as it is completely surrounded by Detroit. In a sense, Dodge Main was a city unto itself almost completely surrounded by Hamtramck. The collaboration between Hamtramck and the Dodge factory goes back to 1910, when John and Horace Dodge came to the then village of Hamtramck looking for a place to build a factory. They already had a factory in downtown Detroit where they manufactured parts for Henry Ford. But that plant was too small, and it was stuffed into a place that was too crowded. Besides, they had bigger ideas. They wanted to build their own cars that would compete with Henry Ford.

Hamtramck seemed to meet their needs perfectly. It was located outside of Detroit, so taxes were lower. It was largely rural, so there was a lot of space to expand, and there were two railroad lines that looped around the factory, with one of them running up the western side of Hamtramck leading directly to Ford's massive factory that he had just opened in the neighboring city of Highland Park.

It looked perfect. They bought a piece of land and began construction in June 1910, and by November 1910, they had some buildings up and had started the manufacturing process. Early on, they put out the word that they needed workers. This call was answered in an incredible fashion as thousands of immigrants, mainly Poles, flooded into the area, drawn by the promise of good jobs (relatively speaking) that paid enough to allow the workers to raise a family in a modest but decent house. In reality, the housing stock in Hamtramck was pretty dreadful. Typically, a new house was equipped with cold running water and electricity. There was no furnace, although there might be a wood- or coal-burning stove, but no hot water and no toilet. That was in the shed out back. Still, it wasn't much worse than what they had left behind in Poland.

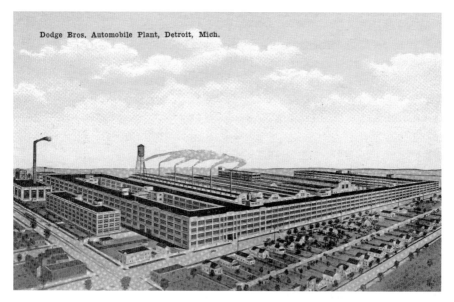

Within a few years of its opening in 1910, the Dodge plant grew to gigantic proportions. And it continued to expand almost until it was demolished seven decades later.

And Dodge Main grew. Guided by Detroit's prince of architects Albert Kahn and the Hinchman & Gryllis architectural firm, the Dodge factory attained impressive dimensions. The main offices and powerhouse went up alongside Jos. Campau Avenue. The main assembly building flanked the south end of the complex. Behind and pushing all the way to Conant Avenue, some one thousand feet to the east, the massive complex eventually consisted of about thirty-five buildings, some rising eight stories tall. It would come to have two massive side-by-side assembly buildings, each one thousand feet long. And a new colossal power plant dominated by four gigantic smokestacks was built at the southeast corner of the complex.

Both Dodge brothers died in 1920, one supposedly from the effects of the 1918 flu pandemic, and the other from drinking too much, with at least part of that due to grief over the loss of his brother. Yet that did nothing to hamper the life of the behemoth they had created. Dodge Main, as it came to be called after it was acquired by the Chrysler Corporation, had become a living entity unto itself. The minute humans who flowed down its aisles, cavernous corridors and winding tunnels were like blood cells breathing life into the concrete and steel.

By World War II, Dodge Main had its own fire department, a huge workers' dining room, a laundry and much more. During this period, it employed forty-five thousand people, making it nearly as large as all of Hamtramck had been population-wise in 1920. Physically, the site was expanded through the years as it absorbed Bismarck Street on the south and rail lines on the north. In all, it had occupied nearly 5 million square feet of floor space. That is nearly double the size of the GM Detroit-Hamtramck Assembly plant that replaced it in 1981, although the Dodge plant footprint was about 135 acres, compared to the GM plant area, which is almost twice the size.

Through its years of operation—1910 to 1979—Dodge Main exerted a tremendous influence on the people who worked there. For some, it was a savior that allowed them to support their families. For others, it was hell. Working conditions were often brutal, with temperatures soaring well above one hundred degrees Fahrenheit on summer days. And the legend is true— on hot summer days, the Dodge brothers did bring in beer to comfort the workers. It could also be a dangerous place. Workers were killed on a regular basis as they were crushed by machinery, electrocuted or were victims of some other accident. Even worse, crime and corruption flourished in some factories, especially those in the inner-city areas in the 1960s and 1970s, when there seemed to be a general societal breakdown. Drug deals were done from lockers, hookers worked the assembly lines, loan sharks carried

At its peak of operations during World War II, Dodge Main was made up of about thirty-five buildings, some one thousand feet long, covering 135 acres. And it employed more than forty-five thousand people.

bundles of cash in their pockets and you just might look out a window and watch your car being stolen from the factory parking lot below. Workers often carried guns, and arguments could be settled amid the roar of machinery that drowned out gunshots.

It happened more than once at Dodge Main. In fact, it happened twice in one week in late January and early February 1973. Hopes for a bloodless year—there had been three homicides in the city in 1972—were crushed early, when Waverly T. Lucas was shot in the head and shoulder in the plant on a Thursday evening.

According to a witness Waverly, who was working the afternoon shift, was walking down a fifth-floor passageway at about 8:30 p.m., when he was approached by two men. He spoke with them for a short while, and a scuffle began. Then one of the men pulled a gun and shot Waverly. Both men then fled into a maze of corridors in the plant. Waverly was taken to nearby Henry Ford Hospital, where he died shortly after arrival.

The deep, dark depths of Dodge Main provided the environment that could help conceal an attacker.

Police theorized that Waverly was the victim of a robbery, since some money had been taken from his pockets. His wife told police that Waverly had worked at the plant for twenty years and didn't have any enemies that she knew of. But she noted that her husband "seemed kind of worried the last three or four weeks."

Two suspects were arrested, but no charges were filed for lack of evidence.

Eight days after Waverly was killed in Dodge Main, a second man was shot to death. But this time there was no question of who did it. John Holston, sixty, got into an argument with Fred Pierson as both were working on the assembly line. Holston claimed that Pierson used a crane to create an opening on the assembly line, disrupting the flow. That escalated into an argument, and Holston shot Pierson in the right side. Pierson was also taken to Henry Ford Hospital, where he died.

Holston was arraigned in Hamtramck Municipal Court. Police said the shooting of Pierson was not related to the killing of Waverly the week before.

And can a building be held accountable for murder? Not likely, but if it could, just about every factory everywhere would face charges. Many died in those walls, usually by accidents, crushed by falling equipment, electrocuted, drowned in chemicals, burned by faulty equipment and more. And consider the case of Ed Bannik, who was one of five employees overcome by a two-week heat wave. All five worked at the Dodge Main factory in the days before air conditioning became common. And all five were taken to St. Francis Hospital for treatment. Bannik died an hour after he arrived at the hospital.

Although no one went to jail, working conditions at the factories were, indeed, murder.

Case 1970-1

Homicide

The 1970s had barely begun when Hamtramck recorded its first murder of the year (and decade if you accept January 1, 1970, not 1971, as the first day of the decade). Matthew Burke, thirty-three, the owner of Burke's Bar at 7727 Jos. Campau Avenue, across from the Dodge Main factory, was shot as he attempted to flee from armed robbers.

Burke had driven his car into the parking lot next to the bar, when he was accosted by three robbers who grabbed him and hit him in the face with a gun as he got out of his car. Burke broke free and ran toward the bar, where there was an open window. Burked tried to escape the robbers by jumping into the bar through the window, but one of the robbers fired, striking Burke in chest with a .45-caliber round. He collapsed on the floor inside and was immediately followed by the robbers.

A bartender tried to come to Burke's aid but was stopped by one of the robbers, who pointed a gun at him. "Stay where you are," the robber ordered. He did. One of the robbers picked up a canvas bag containing $3,490 that Burke had been carrying and fled to a waiting car that sped off.

They didn't get far, though. Police were able to trace the getaway car. Detroit police joined in the hunt as the car's owner, Elgin Hall, thirty-one, lived in Detroit. They placed his house under observation until he was spotted coming home a couple days after the robbery. He was arrested, and police said it would only be a matter of a few days until the other two men were captured.

The daytime street-side murder of Burke shook up the local business community, leading Chief Arthur Chojnacki to weigh bolstering police protection. "I am considering the possibility of offering a uniformed escort to merchants when they are carrying large sums of money," he said. But it never happened.

CASE 1975-1

Homicide

It took four men to murder Katherine DiLorenzo, twenty-five, in her home on Holbrook Street in January 1975, and, still, they managed to get captured a few hours after the crime.

One of the four included her estranged husband, but he wasn't there when she was shot. Philip Jacoy, Michael Agbay and Ronald Ferguson, all of Detroit, were. They had been hired by her husband, James DiLorenzo, to carry out the shooting. And they did on January 18, 1975, when Jacoy and Ferguson claimed to be St. Clair Shores plainclothes policemen. They used that ruse to get into her home and then Jacoy shot Katherine in her living room. Her mother was nearby. Both men fled to a waiting car, which was driven away by Agbay.

But somebody got the license plate number of the car, and the three were tracked down by Detroit police in a matter of hours. Jacoby was sentenced to life in prison. Agbay and Ferguson got ten to fifteen years. James DiLorenzo was first charged with first-degree murder but agreed to a deal and pleaded guilty to a lesser charge of manslaughter.

CASE 1977-1

One of the most memorable years in Hamtramck's history was 1977.

But it was for the worst wrong reason. That year, Hamtramck marked a record nine homicides, including a triple murder.

The year arrived innocently. The Federal Economic Development Agency rejected the city's request for more money for public works programs (no surprise there), the public library dedicated a bicentennial room to house memorabilia from the previous year's celebrations and Joe Hudson was named the new principal at Hamtramck High School. These were just the kinds of stories that made newspaper readers yawn. The good times ended pretty quickly, though, with the year's first killing, which technically was a homicide but legally was classified as manslaughter.

It happened in the early morning hours of Sunday, February 13, 1977, when Willie Douglas Buck of Detroit was shot and killed by a store owner outside the Johnny's Pizza parlor at 2936 Caniff Street. But don't weep too hard for Buck. He was shot while toting a sawed-off shotgun, with which he was attempting to rob the store owner. Police said the store owner was working inside at about 12:30 a.m., when an employee alerted him that there were two men acting suspiciously outside. The owner went out to watch over the delivery cars used by employees. It was common for them to keep the cars running when picking up pizzas ready for home delivery. The owner was concerned because there had been a number of car thefts in recent months. As the owner leaned against the side of an adjacent building, the two men approached him. Buck pointed the shotgun at him and said, "This is a hold-up. Let's get inside." As the owner turned to face them, he reached into his belt, where he had a gun. He pulled it and fired at the men, striking Buck in the lower chest. Buck fell and then tried to lift his head and point the gun at the store owner, who said, "Don't do it or I'll shoot," and ran into the store to call police. They found Buck with the gun tied around his neck with shoelaces.

The owner had a permit to carry the gun, which was registered with police. The Wayne County prosecutor ruled that the shooting was "justifiable."

CASE NO. 1977-2

Homicide

A mysterious stranger was sought by police after the stabbing of a twenty-year-old woman who was babysitting her friend's three children. But who was he? Did he actually do it? And why? No one knows.

The victim was Patricia Forton, who was babysitting at her friend's house on Trowbridge Street. Forton was a former employee of North Detroit General Hospital at the Hamtramck-Detroit border. She was five months pregnant at the time of her death.

Unravelling the story of her death was a challenging task for police, for much of it didn't seem to make sense. What they did piece together was this: At about 11:30 p.m. on Thursday, April 21, Forton was sitting on the front porch of her friend's house. The kids, an eight-year-old and two-year-old twins, were inside sleeping. A man, described as about thirty years old, came walking by. He was carrying a bottle of wine in a paper bag. He asked Forton for a glass of water, saying he was feeling dizzy. She complied and brought a glass of water from inside the house. He then said he had a headache and asked for an aspirin. She brought him one. Police know these details because Forton's friend returned home at about 1:30 a.m. and found Forton and the man sitting in the living room, talking. The three spoke for about an hour and then the friend suggested the man leave. She went into the kitchen to use the phone to call a cab for him. While making the call, she heard Forton scream that she had been stabbed. As the friend returned to the living room, she saw the man running from the house. Forton staggered into the bathroom, where she collapsed, and that's where police found her. They recovered the knife and the bottle of wine the man had.

The friend told police that she thought at first that Forton knew him, but she said Forton said she didn't. Supporting the claim that there even was a man was a police report that someone fitting the description of the man was seen going door to door that evening.

So, who was he, and why did he kill her?

He was never tracked down, so it's likely we will never know.

CASE 1977-3

Homicide

He was "a nice fella, never in trouble, hard working, the son of a minister and a church-going mother." That was how police detective Larry Pietrzak described Benjamin Lee Odom, twenty, following his arrest for shooting Quinton McAlpine, twenty-one, of Detroit.

The shooting took place shortly after 11:00 p.m. on Tuesday, May 3, 1977, on Edwin Street, near Odom's house. Odom and McAlpine had gotten into an argument, and McAlpine went after Odom, who ran to his house, a short distance away. There he got a .38-caliber snubnose revolver and fired it at McAlpine just as police were driving nearby. They heard the shot and raced down the street, where they found that McAlpine had been shot once in the leg and again in the head at close range.

McAlpine was taken to North Detroit General Hospital a short distance away, where he died about six hours later. Odom was charged with second-degree murder. McAlpine was known to police. He had been charged in the shooting death of the manager of a grocery store in Detroit the year before but was acquitted.

Case 1977-4, 5, 6

Homicides

One of the most alarming homicides recorded in Hamtramck took place at about 8:30 p.m. on Friday, July 29, 1977. It was alarming, considering the number of victims, the degree of violence, the brazenness of the shooters and the fact that the police had virtually no chance of solving the crime. Further, they were worried that this was just the beginning of a family feud that could get a lot uglier—and bloodier.

The scene was Dave's Coney Island on Jos. Campau Avenue on the south side of town near the viaduct. It wasn't the most charming place. Haphazard signs were plastered on the front wall advertising "Chili," "Hot Dogs," "Coffee" and "Pool." Between the signs, graffiti marred the façade.

The name of the place itself was misleading. Whoever Dave was, he was long gone from this place, which was owned by Nosh Lulgjuraj, a member of the Albanian community that was immigrating to Hamtramck in significant numbers in the 1970s. In fact, everyone involved in the shooting was Albanian. That would add new dimensions to the investigation, for better and worse.

First the facts. Lena Gjonaj, forty-two, was a hothead. He had a reputation for rowdiness and sported a gun, although no one took him too seriously. But on the night of the shooting, he was deadly serious. The troubles actually began the night before, when Gjonaj got into an argument with cousins Mark and George (Djerdj) Sinishtaj, whom he accused of cheating at a card game. Gjonaj then supposedly got into a fight with a friend of the Sinishtajs at the Coney Island at about 4:30 p.m. on Friday. About an hour later, he got into an argument with the brother of the restaurant's owner, Nosh Lulgjuraj. He pulled a rifle from under the counter and fired a shot into the ceiling. Gjonaj left, vowing to go home and get a gun as he threatened to kill the Sinishtajs.

He did return, at about 8:30 p.m., and he was armed with a big gun, possibly a .357 magnum and a small derringer pistol. There were nearly thirty people in the Coney Island at the time, and Gjonaj ordered them out of the restaurant and onto the street. He then turned to George Shinishtaj. George raised his arms to his heads and told Gjonaj to go ahead and shoot him if he wanted. He began to turn his back to Gjonaj, and Gjonaj fired, striking him once in the back. George fell into the arms of his cousin Mark, and Gjonaj shot four more times, striking both men in the back. It isn't

Dave's Coney Island (or Peck's Coney Island, you pick the name) was the site of a wild shootout that left three people dead. Even for the wicked '70s, that was out of hand.

clear exactly what happened next, but Gjonaj apparently walked out of the restaurant and crossed Jos. Campau Avenue, and he was then struck by a single shot that hit him in the armpit, killing him. A witness told police that Gjonaj had shot himself, but that was dismissed by police. Detective Alan Shulgon said, "It's pretty difficult for us to believe that. We're 99 percent sure that it wasn't suicide." Instead, they began a search for a car that was seen speeding off just after the shot was fired. But that was going to be difficult. There were about forty people present at the shooting, but none admitted to seeing anything. This was a family matter, which meant this would be settled according to traditions going back to the Old Country. On the plus side, even if there was retaliation between the families involved, it likely would not involve anyone else in the community, unless some bystander was accidentally targeted.

Ultimately, none were, and however the matter was settled, the police and general public were not involved.

CASE NO. 1977-7

Homicide

The cold-blooded shooting of Devaughn G. Frye was clearly premeditated. At about 1:15 a.m. on Sunday, December 4, 1977, Frye was sleeping in a Trowbridge Street house with his girlfriend, when the girlfriend heard a voice at the door. She recognized the voice as belonging to a friend and opened the door. A second woman was standing outside the door, and behind her was a man armed with a rifle and pistol. According to police, the man asked the girlfriend, "Where's your old man?" The girlfriend indicated the bedroom, and he went there, where Frye was in bed.

The man told Frye to get up twice, but he looked up and turned his head. The man then shot Frye once in the back of the head. The man and the other woman fled from the house, and the girlfriend went downstairs and called police. The suspected killer himself was shot in the head six months later while being chased by police from the city of Allen Park.

CASES NO. 1977-8, 9

Homicides

Just for the record, Hamtramck's eighth homicide of the year involved a woman in the connection of the death of her baby. The ninth capped the worst year ever, with the death of a man who was found lying in a pool of blood in his house on Jacob Street. There were signs of robbery, and suspected drugs were found in the house.

CASE NO. 1978-1

Homicide Ruled Accidental

The next year, 1978, was better but not by much.

The city's finances were tenuous at best, the Michigan Department of Education gave the public school system low marks relating to student academic achievement and the crime rate took off like a rocket. For heaven's sake, it got so bad that someone broke into and ransacked the St. Ladislaus nuns' convent on Caniff Street.

Although 1978 did not live up to 1977's dismal homicide tally, it still recorded five. The first occurred on Friday, February 3, but it wasn't a murder. It was a tragic mistake. A sixteen-year-old girl living on Carpenter Street was shot by her boyfriend of two years. He told police that he had picked up a rifle that was standing in the corner of a room and it immediately fired, striking her. Police arrested the boyfriend, but charges were later dropped by the county prosecutor's office for insufficient evidence. The shooting was ruled accidental, as an examination of the gun showed that a bullet had been jammed in its barrel, leading to the accidental firing.

Case No. 1978-2

Homicide

The second homicide occurred when a twenty-two-year-old Dearborn Heights woman was shot in a house on Faber Street on April 4. A twenty-seven-year-old man was arrested, but police wouldn't say what the motive was.

Case No. 1978-3

Homicide

It was a game of whose body is it, anyway? as Hamtramck and Detroit police scratched their collective heads over who was tagged with the murder that crossed city lines. The killing took place at about 11:00 a.m. on June 29, 1978, in front of the old United Auto Workers Local 262 Union Hall on St. Aubin Street.

Police said that John Henry Jordan of Detroit was walking down the street as a man and woman followed behind. He turned into a parking lot, still followed by the couple, when the man pulled a gun and shot at him. Jordan began to run, but the gunman fired several more times, striking Jordan in the back. Detroit and Hamtramck police responded and realized that they

The line where the grass meets the sidewalk marks the border between Hamtramck and Detroit on St. Aubin Street. Hamtramck is to the right, and Detroit is to the left. That mattered in the investigation of the murder of Henry Jordan in 1978.

had a jurisdictional issue. It didn't impede the investigation, but the case was ultimately turned over to Detroit cops for follow-up. Technically, Jordan was killed in Detroit, just inches from the border line, because the city of Hamtramck ends at the edge of the sidewalk. There is no word if the couple was ever found.

CASE NO. 1978-4

Homicide

Neighbors can be unneighborly, even deadly.

Such was the case of Jean Scott, forty-six, and her neighbor Carol Hicks, forty, who lived on Oklahoma Street at the Col Hamtramck Homes public housing project. The two apparently had been arguing about a drainage problem between their housing units. A witness told police that Scott came to Hicks's apartment to ask him to take her to a store downtown so that she could cash a check and do some shopping. The two began arguing again, and it carried over to outside the unit, where Scott pulled a four-inch knife from her purse and stabbed Hicks several times, the witness said.

The witness disarmed her, and the police were called. Hicks was taken to St. Joseph Mercy Hospital, suffering from stab wounds in the shoulder and left arm. She died at 4:05 a.m. the following morning. Scott was charged with second-degree murder.

CASE NO. 1978-NEVER MIND

Homicide/Kidnapping

The victim's name was Jimmy Hoffa. You might have heard of him. He was president of the International Brotherhood of Teamsters, a fairly substantial labor union. You can learn a lot more about the colorful life of Jimmy Hoffa in a host of books, magazines, websites and even movies. But one thing no one can—or will—tell you is what ever happened to him. We do know that he had plans to return as head of the union following his release from prison in 1971, after serving four years of a thirteen-year sentence for jury tampering, attempted bribery and more. As he tried to position himself to take back the leadership of the Teamsters, he apparently antagonized the organized crime figures who had become associated with the group.

It all came to an end on July 30, 1975, when Hoffa went to have lunch with reputed mobster Anthony Giacalone at the Machus Red Fox restaurant in Bloomfield Township, about fifteen miles north of Detroit. Hoffa drove his green Pontiac Grand Ville to the restaurant at about 1:15 p.m. But Giacalone never showed up. Several people reported seeing Hoffa in the parking lot of the restaurant. One person reported seeing Hoffa in the back of a car with three other people. That was the last that anybody besides his killers saw of him. He disappeared and thus began one of the longest missing person searches in history (aside from the fact that someone is still looking for Cleopatra's corpse).

Since that day, all kinds of theories have been put forward about the location of his remains. From a farm field to a football field to the footings of a building, it's been proposed that he was everywhere—even in Hamtramck.

It was in the parking lot of the Machus Red Fox restaurant in Bloomfield Township that Jimmy Hoffa was last seen on July 30, 1975. Although there was a report that Hoffa's body ended up in Hamtramck, it was never substantiated. A different restaurant now occupies the site.

Yup, Hamtramck. The theory was stated by author Steven Brill in his book *The Teamsters*. He proposed that Hoffa's body was brought to the city for disposal at a local sanitation plant. The theory hit the news and Hamtramckans in September 1978. The FBI said nope. It said that it had never asked for a search warrant for the building and that it had never been searched by any law enforcement agency. It might not have mattered. Part of the building had been destroyed by a fire the previous February. A fire, hmmm…

Anyway, Hoffa, wherever he is, was declared legally dead in 1982.

EULOGY

Murders have occurred in Hamtramck since 1978 and still do to this day, but out of sensitivity to survivors, family members and friends, we will stop our survey here. We've covered a lot of ground and touched on a wide spectrum of murders and motives and just general madness.

So what does it all mean?

Life is cheap. Life is precious. Life is everything. Life is nothing. Take it any way you want. But one thing that is clear is that people have been killing each other since time immemorial. Even Otzi, the body that was frozen in Alpine glacier for five thousand years, was a murder victim, as shown by the arrowhead found buried in his chest. You can bet he wasn't the first guy to take an arrow. When gun powder and guns came along, the task of killing your fellow man became even easier. And whether killing is done in the name of God and country or for the cash you have in your pocket, it still amounts to the same thing. Someone is dead.

Murders usually involve multiple victims beyond those who are shot or stabbed or whatever. There are survivors left behind to mourn the loss of loved ones. They often suffer wounds that never heal. Even the perpetrators might end up dead, executed by society or killed in the commission of their crime. Yet none of that seems to have an effect on the murder rate. Those who studied or even observed crime have noticed that the criminals often give no thought to the consequences of their actions. They live and act for the moment. They have one single-minded purpose, and in the case of murder, that is to kill their victims. The thought of spending life in prison or being executed doesn't enter into the picture. Nor does the pain that the survivors suffer. All that matters is that the person they want dead is dead. What comes after that can be dealt with later.

After reading through these pages and understanding that the murders depicted here are not all that have been committed in the town, one might get the impression that Hamtramck is hopelessly violent. After all, many towns go for decades without recording a single murder. But that is misleading, when you consider the circumstances of this amazing community. Hamtramck is a small town in terms of physical area—2.1 square miles— but its history might be unique in America. This is a town that went from a small farming village to a major industrial city in little more than a decade. This is a town that crowded as many as fifty-six thousand people at one time in its 2.1 square miles. The density was overwhelming, and cramming that many people together in such a small space put a tremendous strain on the residents. Also, rampant poverty, especially during the Great Depression, pushed people to the edge of reason. That was shown not just with the murders but also the suicide rate. None of that justified murder, but it does give a perspective on why such terrible acts occurred, at least in some cases.

Ultimately, Hamtramck's reputation is in the hands of Hamtramckans. That reality will do absolutely nothing to deter future homicides. Reason has no meaning to murderers. So, the city will go on, no doubt recording murders from time to time. But it will survive. And to those who have made their way to these pages, we can only say,

Rest in Peace

ABOUT THE AUTHOR

Greg Kowalski spent more than forty years as a journalist reporting for and editing numerous newspapers and magazines—and covering the occasional murder. He is the executive director of the Hamtramck Historical Museum in Hamtramck. He has written twelve books, ten on Hamtramck.

Visit us at
www.historypress.com
···